KEY TEXTS

THOEMMES

Printed and bound by
Antony Rowe Ltd., Chippenham, Wiltshire

Classic Studies in the History of Ideas

PHILOSOPHY
Its Scope and Relations

Henry Sidgwick

This edition published by Thoemmes Press, 1998

Thoemmes Press
11 Great George Street
Bristol BS1 5RR, England

US office: *Distribution and Marketing*
22883 Quicksilver Drive
Dulles, Virginia 20166, USA

ISBN 1 85506 559 2

This is a reprint of the 1902 edition

Publisher's Note

The publisher has gone to great lengths to ensure the quality of this reprint but points out that some imperfections in the original book may be apparent.

PHILOSOPHY

ITS SCOPE AND RELATIONS

AN INTRODUCTORY COURSE OF LECTURES

BY THE LATE

HENRY SIDGWICK

KNIGHTBRIDGE PROFESSOR OF MORAL PHILOSOPHY IN THE
UNIVERSITY OF CAMBRIDGE

London
MACMILLAN AND CO., Limited
NEW YORK: THE MACMILLAN COMPANY
1902

All rights reserved

EDITORIAL NOTE

SOME three months before his death, when he knew that his illness was likely to be fatal, Professor Sidgwick asked the editor to take charge of certain of his uncompleted works which he thought might be found suitable for publication. About the same time he dictated an account of them and made various suggestions in writing concerning their treatment, substantially repeating what he had before said in person. The present book he described as "a course of eleven lectures, together with three printed lectures, in which I attempt to define the scope of Philosophy and its relation to other studies, especially Psychology, Logic, History, etc." "This," he adds, "I judge might with advantage be published. It wants revision. In the earlier part there would be some difficulty in fitting in the printed lectures with the oral comments on them, and in the later part there are some repetitions which would have to be cut out."

Professor Sidgwick had long ago planned such an introduction to the study of philosophy. In 1892 he delivered a short course of lectures bearing the title of the present work. These, considerably expanded, were repeated as *Elements of Philosophy* (*Theoretical and Practical*) in the two following years. In 1897 he began working up this material, and three lectures, dealing severally with the Scope of Philosophy, its Relation to Psychology, and the Scope of Metaphysics, were privately printed. But his further progress was temporarily—and, as it has proved, was permanently—interrupted in consequence of his undertaking to deliver in 1898 and onwards the complete course of lectures on 'Metaphysics,' as specified in the syllabus of the Moral Sciences Tripos. Though called 'Metaphysics,' the subject as outlined there is really in the main Epistemology; and there is little doubt that the more detailed treatment of the Theory of Knowledge, which this change of work involved, would have been turned to account, had Professor Sidgwick been able to resume the preparation of his Philosophy.

To the students attending this 'Metaphysics' course copies of the lectures already printed were distributed, and the first five lectures of the course were occupied in supplementing and elucidating these—the whole by way of introduction before entering upon the study of the special questions and text-books prescribed. Out of this material, that is to say the three printed lectures and five manuscript lectures referred to in Professor Sidgwick's statement as "the earlier part," Lectures I.-V. of this book as it stands have been made up. Only a few of the printed sentences have been omitted: these have been replaced by fuller expositions in manuscript that seemed obviously meant to supersede them. But from the written lectures the omissions have been more extensive, 'oral comments' being here frequent that were plainly intended only to serve a temporary purpose. Lecture V. is unfortunately very incomplete: the special topic of which it treats—the Relation of Metaphysics to Epistemology—was reached only at the very end of the last printed lecture, and even in the corresponding manuscript lecture it is but cursorily handled. In fact this topic was one appropriate to a later stage in the course of lectures on Metaphysics, to which the earlier part of this book served as an introduction: the fuller treatment was therefore naturally deferred. Professor Sidgwick was himself well aware of this defect and suggested that "perhaps some assistance might be derived" from using certain portions of the Metaphysics course which he goes on to mention. But this course assumes the constant use of particular text-books—Kant's *Critique*, his *Prolegomena*, Sigwart's *Logic*, and several others— and detailed references to these are frequent: without re-casting and in part re-writing them, portions of such lectures could hardly be fitly incorporated in a book like the present. One passage has, however, been inserted as an Appendix to Lecture V.: to attempt more has not seemed wise. On p. 103 it is proposed in subsequent lectures to examine the Transcendentalism of the late Professor T. H. Green. This was done later on in the Metaphysics course; and possibly this criticism may find a place in a volume of philosophical remains which, it is hoped, may be published hereafter.

In what Professor Sidgwick called "the later part," Lectures VI.-XI. that is to say, the editor was only advised to cut out repetitions. Nevertheless some of these, and in particular the *resumés* with which these lectures usually begin, have been allowed to remain; for the re-statement is often further statement, and excision without mutilation or foreign interpolation was in some cases not possible. As 'the earlier part' of the original *Elements of Philosophy* (*Theoretical and Practical*) was used separately as an introduction to the advanced lectures on Metaphysics, so this later part was used separately—apparently with considerable additions—in a course entitled *Philosophy and Sociology*, delivered in 1896 and again in 1898. The original *Elements* had concluded with three lectures on the Scope and Divisions of Practical Philosophy and its Relation to Theoretical Philosophy. Now it will be found that on p. 27 there is a reference to a subsequent discussion of the relation of Ethics to Politics; and again on p. 94 a further treatment "of the problem presented by the relation of Theoretical to Practical Philosophy" is promised. Yet no mention was made of these topics in the brief statements Professor Sidgwick had dictated, nor were the MSS. of the lectures themselves among those he had put together as belonging to this book. Two of them were, however, discovered after some search among his ethical papers. One, in which the relation of Ethics and Politics is discussed, is too fragmentary for publication;[1] but the concluding lecture dealing with the Relation of Theoretical to Practical Philosophy it has been thought well to include here, since its separation from the rest can be explained by what has been said, and since, further, the passages cited seem to negative the supposition that its omission was intentional. It appears accordingly—solely on the editor's responsibility—as Lecture XII.

In Lecture V. the author has made use of a few passages from an article on the 'Criteria of Truth and Error' contributed to

[1] A discussion of this question will be found in the *Methods of Ethics*, bk. i., ch. ii., and also in the *Elements of Politics*, ch. xiii.

Mind, January 1900; and in Lectures VI.-IX. he has worked up the greater part of an article on the 'Historical Method' contributed to *Mind*, April 1886; some paragraphs of Lecture XII. had also appeared previously in the *Proceedings of the Aristotelian Society*.

Throughout the book what few editorial additions there are—other than references and the division into sections—will be found enclosed in square brackets. The lecture form has been retained, and none but small and obvious verbal changes have been made; because the editor's aim throughout has been simply to place the author's work before the reader as he left it. The attempt by emendation and addition to approximate to what the work would have been had the author himself been permitted to finish it, would—the reader will probably allow—have been an unwarrantable liberty even in one who felt confident of his competence for the task.

Special thanks are due to Mr. G. C. Rankin, Scholar of Trinity College, for valuable help in preparing the lectures for press and in compiling the Table of Contents: he has also provided the Index. The proofs have all been carefully read over by Mrs. Sidgwick: innumerable corrections are due wholly to her.

JAMES WARD.

Trinity College, Cambridge,
March 12, 1902.

CONTENTS

LECTURE I

THE SCOPE OF PHILOSOPHY

PAGES

1. PHILOSOPHY should have a meaning (1) clear, (2) useful, and (3) *as far as possible* in conformity with common usage. It is to be distinguished from Science, Psychology, Epistemology, etc. 1–4
2. While the Sciences attend to particular parts of the knowable world, Philosophy aims at putting them together into a systematic whole. It may be said that Science is concerned only with *phenomena*, while Philosophy seeks to know the Realities underlying them. But Science, too, is concerned with Reality, and Philosophy cannot ignore phenomena. . 4–17
3. Mr. Spencer defines Philosophy as *completely* unified knowledge, but this definition overlooks the fact that essential difference in the nature of the whole is as important as resemblance; and his own doctrine of Evolution illustrates this defect. . 17–20

LECTURE II

THE SCOPE OF PHILOSOPHY (*continued*)

1. Philosophy must deal with the principles and methods of determining 'what ought to be' as well as with those concerning 'what is': its unifying function thus includes not only the 'positive sciences,' but also Ethics, Politics, etc. . . 21–25
2. It is the business of *Ethics* to treat of details of duty or right conduct, but Ethical *Philosophy* is primarily concerned with the general principles and methods of moral reasoning. A similar distinction may be applied to Politics. Practical Philosophy is thus a supreme architectonic study aiming at the complete systematisation of Arts and Ends: its position

relatively to these is analogous to that of Theoretical Philosophy to Science in general. 25–30

3. The final task of Philosophy is to co-ordinate these two divisions of its subject-matter. Here a difficult problem arises—the relation of Philosophy to Religion (see Appendix at the end of the lecture).

Regarded as ends having a certain value and relative importance, the several sciences and even Theoretical Philosophy itself seem subordinate to Practical Philosophy; but this, on the other hand, regarded as a system of judgments or beliefs belongs to that cognisable existence with which Theoretical Philosophy deals. Philosophy, then, in its widest sense aims at comprehending all rational thought as one coherent whole. 30–35

4. Hence, since everything that we know or believe, whether concerning 'what is' or 'what ought to be,' is necessarily thought about, it becomes a problem to distinguish the matter of Philosophy from the matter of Psychology. . 35–37

APPENDIX—Relation of Philosophy to Religion. . . . 38–40

LECTURE III

THE RELATION OF PHILOSOPHY TO PSYCHOLOGY

1. Adopting provisionally the Common Sense distinction of Mind and Matter, we see that Mind may be considered either (1) in itself, or (2) in relation to Matter. The relation of Philosophy and Psychology to be examined from both these points of view. 41–45

2. With feelings and feeling-prompted volitions Philosophy has no special concern: only in thoughts and reasoned purposes has it common ground with Psychology. But there is a Psychological Philosophy, according to which the former are the elements of which the latter are composed: this, like Materialistic Philosophy, is a paradoxical divergence from Common Sense, but in an opposite direction.

Philosophy is concerned primarily with truth, Psychology with the false and the true alike. But even in dealing with true beliefs, the methods of Psychology and Philosophy differ —the one seeks, introspectively, to ascertain their actual development; the other, dialectically, their ideal order and connexion. 45–51

3. As to the relation of mind to the material world, the complete disparateness of mental facts and nervous changes forbids their treatment as two 'faces of the same thing.' Their causal *nexus* is the important problem, but one that belongs to Philosophy: Psycho-physiology may content itself with ascertaining their concomitance.

CONTENTS

But there is a second and quite different relation of mind to matter—that of the cognition that has matter for its object. 51-60
4. Out of the double relation of mind to matter arise the contrasted systems of Materialism and Mentalism—the one identifying thought or feeling with the concomitant nerve-process, the other analysing matter as an object of perception into mental elements. Materialism may be dismissed as loose and confused, but Mentalism requires examination. We note three types of it, Phenomenalism, Sensationalism, and Idealism.

In examining the analysis of our cognition of matter three different methods are to be distinguished: (a) *Reflective Analysis* resolving this cognition into secondary qualities and relational qualities of extension and incompressibility; (b) *Psychogonical Analysis* hypothetically tracing back this combination of percepts and concepts to association of sensational 'elements.' 60-70
5. But such 'elements' are in truth only antecedents, and the reality of matter as *concomitant* of mental changes is assumed, as naïvely as it is by Common Sense, throughout this analysis of matter as *object* perceived. The question whether (c) *Transcendental Analysis* can overthrow Natural Dualism to be considered later. 70-75

LECTURE IV

THE SCOPE OF METAPHYSICS

1. In considering the relation to Mind of Matter as an object of thought we are drawn into Metaphysics. To determine its scope we must survey the marginal studies from which it is more or less vaguely distinguished, viz. Physics, Philosophy, Psychology, and Logic. 76-82
2. The propositions of Physics are always somehow capable of 'empirical verification' and may thus be provisionally distinguished from those of Metaphysics; the progress of knowledge may, however, bring within the range of physical inquiry questions that are now left to the metaphysician. . . 82-86
3. Similarly, and with a like reservation, we may differentiate Metaphysics from Empirical Psychology. . . . 86-87
4. Similarly, too, Philosophy, so far as the synthesis of the knowable at which it aims is capable—directly or indirectly—of verification by particular experiences, is *Non-Metaphysical* Philosophy; whereas Metaphysics inquires what, if anything, can be known *à priori* 87-91
5. According to this criterion—verification by particular experiences—Transcendentalism, which attempts to determine the neces-

sary conditions of experience by reflection on experience as a whole, is metaphysical. 91–93
6. Rational Theology is metaphysical, but knowledge of God's existence being unattainable by observation or experiment, Rational Theology is to be distinguished not from Empirical, but from Revelational, Theology. To it belongs the final and most important problem of Philosophy—the relation of Theoretical and Practical Philosophy. But up to a certain point this problem admits of empirical treatment. . . 94–95
7. Metaphysics has been more positively characterised as Ontology or systematic knowledge of the Real or Absolute as contrasted with knowledge of the Phenomenal or Relative. On this view we may say that Metaphysics includes Ontology, or at least investigates its claims. But it cannot be maintained that science has no concern with reality. And so far the provisional view of verification previously given proves inadequate; for in distinguishing between appearance and reality the criterion is not sense-perception but certain assumptions as to the uniformity of Nature. But how is the validity of these assumptions to be tested? This question brings us to the Relation of Metaphysics and Epistemology, to be dealt with in the next lecture. 95–102
APPENDIX—Transcendentalism and Idealism. . . . 102–104

LECTURE V

THE SCOPE OF METAPHYSICS (*continued*)

1. Some criterion for distinguishing truth from error is a necessary preliminary to the complete unification of knowledge which we have taken to be the business of Philosophy. Such systematised inquiry into what is taken for knowledge may be called Epistemology. 105–110
2. Such 'Theory of Knowledge' is then an aspect or function of Philosophy. But Logic also has the same aim in some measure; how then are Logic and Epistemology to be distinguished? 110–113
3. According to the Kantians Logic gives only the criterion of *formal* truth, and no *general* criterion of material truth is possible . 113–114
4. According to Mill, it gives only the criterion of inferred truth, and particular propositions obtained by direct observation and general propositions obtained by direct intuition are left to be dealt with by Metaphysics. Nevertheless Mill's Logic continually transgresses these narrower limits, and in fact a decisive separation of general Logic (or Methodology) from Epistemology is impracticable. 114–117

CONTENTS xiii

PAGES

5. Nor—so long as Metaphysics is as uncertain as it is—can Epistemology be separated from it, *i.e.* Epistemology must include the investigation of the claims of Ontology. . . . 117–118
APPENDIX—Relation of Epistemology to Ontology. . . 119–121

LECTURE VI

RELATION OF PHILOSOPHY TO HISTORY

1. The so-called 'Historical Method' claims to have 'invaded and transformed all departments of thought.' Taking history to include the study of changes, whether of things or thoughts in the more or less distant past, we have to examine its claims to present, not merely facts in chronological order, but the laws of their development. 122–127
2. The methods and conclusions of mathematics and rational physics cannot be materially affected by the historical method; and the philosophical problem suggested by the actual particularity of the cosmos will remain—however far back our conjectural history may read—just as inexplicable as it is at present. 127–133
3. It is undeniable that Biology has been 'transformed' by an evolutionary or historical method; but it is no less true that the theory of change in the remote past is altogether determined by the conclusions formed by study of the present and recent past. 133-139

LECTURE VII

RELATION OF PHILOSOPHY TO HISTORY (*continued*)

1. Recapitulation of preceding lecture. 140–142
2. The Darwinian theory leaves the philosophical objections to materialism unchanged: the arguments for and against the immortality of the soul are also unaffected by it. The argument against immortality founded on the continuity between soulless and soul-possessing organisms is not really strengthened by the theory of Evolution and is moreover itself invalid. 142–148
3. Some are prepared to admit that sensations may have been completely caused by movements of organic matter, but maintain that 'general notions,' etc., cannot be derived from

sensations. But the greater disparity between psychical facts as a whole and physical facts is against such an admission. We conclude then that the historical method as applied to Anthropology leaves the metaphysical problem of the relation of mind and matter where it was. 148–149

4. The results of the historical method applied to Psychology, or Psychogony, are often misconceived through a confusion already signalised (see Lecture III.) between psychical antecedents and psychical elements. Further, the processes ascertained by this method are distinct from the meaning or validity of their products. Nevertheless it is thought such investigations may affect our estimate of these. . . 149–152

5. This question—how far the validity of beliefs can be thus affected —carries us over into Sociology. The importance of investigating the changes in the beliefs of human societies is undeniable, but the claim of the historical method to undertake the function of Epistemology and determine how far such beliefs are true or false requires examination ; to this we shall pass in the next lecture. 152–156

LECTURE VIII

RELATION OF PHILOSOPHY TO SOCIOLOGY

1. Hitherto we have taken 'history' in the widest sense, as the study of past facts generally : in turning to the narrower study of past *social* facts it is preferable to use the term *Sociological*, rather than Historical, Method. The individual adult man is what he is in consequence of having grown up in social relations, and we have to study the development of the social mind which he shares. . . . 157–162

2. It will be simpler to consider first the *destructive*, and then the *constructive* effect of sociological inquiry into the history of beliefs on our philosophical views of their validity. The actual diversity of successive beliefs in departments of thought such as ethics, politics, and theology, which are still subjects of controversy, tends to a general scepticism as to the validity of any ; but such vague scepticism is mere weakness and without logical justification. 162–167

3. The question still remains whether an examination of the particular antecedents of particular beliefs may not prove their falsity. When demonstrably false opinions are found among the causes of a belief, this may *suggest* its falsity, but will only *prove* it where those opinions are put forward as reasons for the belief. 167–171

CONTENTS

LECTURE IX

RELATION OF PHILOSOPHY TO SOCIOLOGY (*continued*)

                                                                                          PAGES

1. Recapitulation of the preceding lecture. . . . 172–174
2. It is held that the study of the development of opinion will yield a criterion of truth. But it is not shown how knowledge of the laws of such development *alone* could establish the truth of opinion that it is foreseen will hereafter be current. Moreover, if we start by regarding the opinions of our own time as true, then—so far as change is conceived to go on in fundamental beliefs—the past having been a process through error to truth, the future must be conceived as the reverse process; the past can thus hardly give us much insight into it. . 174–178
3. This difficulty is met by saying (1) that 'knowledge is relative' and (2) that knowledge—and society generally—is progressive! But '*Relativism*' does not entirely remove it; since one truth at least is absolutely known—viz. that all truth is relative. The development of the past without, can thus afford little guidance as to that of the future with, this condition. 178–182
4. The philosophical meaning of relativity with which we are here concerned is relativity to the knowing subject, *i.e.* 'the best approximation to truth' attainable by the mind in question. But sociologically what seems meant by relative truth is a belief expedient for the preservation or welfare of society at a given time. But this presupposes that we know wherein the social 'end' consists, and this we cannot learn from Sociology . 182–189

LECTURE X

RELATION OF PHILOSOPHY TO SOCIOLOGY (*continued*)

1. Recapitulation. 190–192
2. We do not, it is said, enter on the study of the history of belief as a social fact with no other criterion than sociology affords. Knowledge is progressive and the philosophic systematisation of the most advanced or positive sciences provides us with an independent criterion enabling us to forecast the progress of those less advanced. 192–195
3. It is desirable to examine *Progressivism* first in relation to society generally. We cannot take social progress to imply any termination, but we may still ask about its direction: Is it towards increased adaptation to the condition of existence? But the changes which history shows have no universal tendency of this kind. 196–205

xvi   PHILOSOPHY

PAGES

4. As to the special case of changes in beliefs, the question is not primarily whether these are in the direction of truth, but whether they are in the direction of increasing the self-preservative quality of the social organism. There is, again, no evidence of such a general tendency. . . . 205–211

LECTURE XI

RELATION OF PHILOSOPHY TO SOCIOLOGY (*continued*)

1. Recapitulation. 212–214
2. Progress in civilisation is, so far as it goes, a gain, even though it does not increase the self-preservative capacity of the particular social organism in which it occurs : also it is a gain that tends to spread to others by imitation and tradition. We cannot then measure social progress by any narrower conception than that of conduciveness to the welfare of humanity at large. 214–216
3. But how are we to determine this conception truly? This question leads us back to the claim of Sociology to establish a criterion of truth (X. § 2). Accepting as types the positive sciences that have finally emerged from the condition of fundamental controversy, we are to learn to develop rightly those that are still in this stage. But the controversies in politics and ethics relate mainly to *ultimate ends*. These are not phenomena, so that to attempt to treat them by a 'positive' instead of a metaphysical method is futile. And even in the positive sciences we find not identity but diversity of methods, and a survey of these gives us no definite guidance in harmonising our judgments concerning ultimate good and evil. 216–221
4. We have next to examine the claim to antiquate Theology. The alleged opposition between its volitional explanations and those of science vanish when the Divine Will is conceived as orderly and so open to investigation. But it is said that Nature as known to science is non-ethical, and it must be allowed that it is opposed to the conception of a perfectly good will. A deeper opposition between Theology and Science is found in the exclusion by the latter of all teleological conceptions. 221–225
5. This alleged antiteleological tendency of science involves conflict not only with Theology but with any metaphysics that retains the notion of End or Good. But in so far as Science expressly limits its inquiries to the phenomenal, it cannot collide with Theology or Metaphysics unless it asserts that nothing else can be known ; and this negation is *not* a scientific conclusion, but the metaphysical dogma of Posi-

CONTENTS

tivism. And even science requires teleological ideas in studying mind. The one important lesson Philosophy has to learn from Science is patience and hope. 225–231

LECTURE XII

RELATION OF THEORETICAL TO PRACTICAL PHILOSOPHY

1. Assuming at the outset that Practical Philosophy has attained to internal coherence and taking 'what ought to be' to include the 'good' and the 'right,' we find from both points of view divergence between this and 'what is.' . 232–235
2. Is this difference irreducible? At least it is not reducible by way of Psychology or Sociology—the attempt either renders ethics meaningless or involves the surreptitious introduction of ethical notions. 235–237
3. Rational Theology is specially concerned with this problem, but fails to work it out. If we ask why God's power does not cause the complete realisation of ideal Right, we are told that Free Will renders the admission of wrong-doing inevitable. But even granting this, physical evil still remains, and there seems to be no way of reconciling this with the goodness of God unless we conceive the Divine Purpose as externally conditioned. 237–241
4. So far we have assumed that Practical Philosophy is in itself coherent; but the conflict of self-interest and duty is against this view. If Theism were self-evident or demonstrable this conflict would disappear. As a reasonable but provisional assumption it may be confirmed by consistency with other like assumptions: if however such assumptions conflict we must infer that some are false. 241–243
5. The postulate of Moral Order is an assumption of this class, and we have now to consider the connexion of Theism and Moral Order. It is generally admitted that we may believe in the latter without Divine Personality. On the other hand (with one exception) the abstract arguments for Theism do not tend to prove Moral Order. 243–245
6. In the world of Duty and the world of Fact, regarded epistemologically, we discover similar relations of thought and the difference between the two from this point of view are of a subordinate kind. In the case of thought about 'what is,' though error may lie in want of correspondence between thought and fact, it can only be exposed by showing inconsistency between thought and thought, as in the case of thought about 'what ought to be.' 245–247

LECTURE I

THE SCOPE OF PHILOSOPHY

§ 1. It is my object, in the present lecture, to define as clearly as possible the meaning of the term 'Philosophy.' To do this thoroughly will take more than one lecture; and perhaps it may be thought that I am spending too much time in talking 'about words.' But a discussion about words is often the most convenient way of bringing before our minds important relations of thought and fact: and it is likely to be specially instructive in dealing with a subject so full of controversy as the present. For controversy usually implies mutual misunderstanding among thinkers: and if we can agree on the meaning of cardinal terms, we shall have done much to avoid misunderstanding. If a thoroughly distinctive and comprehensive definition of the province of Philosophy could be worked out and universally accepted, its acceptance would mean that we were at least agreed on the questions that the philosopher has to ask, if not on the answers that ought to be given to them: and to ask the right questions is, as Aristotle saw, an important step towards obtaining the right answers.

Now in trying to make clear the meaning of a word, the first thing is to distinguish it from, and ascertain its relation to, words that represent cognate ideas; especially when the common usage of two words seems to indicate that their meanings are liable to be confounded. In this case the most obvious word to select for comparison is 'Science': since on the one hand we commonly recognise that the meanings of the two words are not the same, and yet they seem often to be used in an oddly alternative way. Compare, for example, 'Moral Philosophy' and 'Ethical Science,' 'Political Philosophy' and 'Political Science,' 'Mental Philosophy' and 'Mental Science';—in each case the two terms compared seem to be often applied indifferently to the same course of study. These instances may suggest that Philosophy is a general term for a special group of sciences;—what we call 'Moral' sciences. But, firstly, its use is not confined to these. The term 'Natural Philosophy' is still employed—though perhaps with some doubt as to its propriety—as more or less convertible with 'Physics.' Indeed I am told that a distinguished Professor of Physics in a northern university once commenced his lectures by laying down that 'there are two kinds of Philosophy, Natural Philosophy and Unnatural Philosophy'; thus implying not only that Physics has a valid claim to the name of Philosophy, but that there is no other body of *sound* reasoning to which the term is applicable.

And, secondly, we have to observe that the usage of the term 'Philosophy' seems to imply that it is not exactly—like Science—a common name for many different studies with different methods; that, though it may have different parts or branches, these must be connected by a unity of method. Thus, in speaking of 'Schools of Philosophy,' we imply that the characteristics peculiar to each school will be found in all parts of their philosophical teaching: *e.g.* thinkers of the 'empirical school' are supposed to form their conclusions on the basis of experience of particular facts—instead of laying as a foundation general truths—equally when they are arguing about geometrical axioms or the infinity of space and time, and when they are arguing about questions of right and wrong in conduct.

I have said enough to show that if we can obtain a satisfactory definition of Philosophy which will enable us to distinguish it clearly from Science, while at the same time explaining its close affinity to Science, we shall probably avoid some confusion of thought. To this task I now proceed; but it may be well first to explain exactly what I aim at—and hope to attain —in a process of definition.

I wish to give to the term 'Philosophy' a meaning which will be (1) clear, (2) useful—*i.e.* which will denote something that wants a separate name—and (3) *as far as possible* in conformity with common usage. Note that the last aim cannot be attained completely, so far as common usage is confused and varying: *e.g.* so far as Philosophy is confounded with Science. Still I think that here and in other cases we may find distinctions, vaguely and imperfectly recognised in ordinary discourse, which when made clear and explicit will furnish the required definition. So far as usage is vague and varying, it would be futile to aim at complete uniformity with it: but in my view there is a distinction between 'Philosophy' and the subjects otherwise named which I seek to distinguish from it precisely—Science, Psychology, Epistemology, Logic, etc.—which is more or less recognised in the ordinary thought[1] of educated persons and may be made clear by careful reflection.

§ 2. I will first endeavour to distinguish Philosophy from Science.[2] Science is certainly a kind of

---

[1] I say in ordinary thought; I should add 'of the present age.' The word has come down to us from the Greeks, and it is a historical inquiry of some interest to trace the changes of meaning through which the word has passed during more than two thousand years. But it would be confusing, and would render our task more difficult, to mix this historical inquiry with the search for a definition appropriate to our present thought.

[2] And here I must notice a special source of divergence—and sometimes of confusion—in definitions in our subject, which arises from the influence of the German language, through translations, on English thought. Thus in Külpe's definition of Philosophy [Cf. O. Külpe : *Introduction to Philosophy* (Eng. trans.), 1897, ch. 1. This was one of the text-books recommended to his class by Professor Sidgwick.] 'Science' is used in a somewhat different meaning from that which I decide to give to the word. This is partly because the term which the translator renders Science is ' *Wissenschaft*': and ' *Wissenschaft*' has in common German usage, at least to the best of my knowledge and judgment, a somewhat wider meaning than that which 'Science' has in English usage. For instance, I do not consider History a Science, so far as it is merely concerned with presenting particular events in chronological order : and I think this is clearly in accordance with English usage : but I believe that in German, History even in this limited view of it would be regarded as a Wissenschaft. Hence I am not surprised that Külpe decides without hesitation that Philosophy is a 'Wissenschaft'; but I do not hold that to be a sufficient reason for regarding it as a 'Science' according to English usage.

When we speak of 'the Sciences,' we mean what is sometimes more definitely expressed as 'the special sciences'—a group of organised bodies of knowledge: no one doubts that the geometer, physicist, botanist, has attained important knowledge that other men lack who have not studied geometry, physics, botany. Can we say the same of Philosophy?

Not, at any rate, so confidently: some would here object—pressing the derivation of the word—that Philosophy is rather a study, an inquiry, a pursuit, than a kind of knowledge. The philosopher, they would say, 'loves wisdom,' but it does not follow that he possesses, or ever will possess, what he loves. It may be that he is in pursuit of an object which continually recedes as he pursues:—an ideal whose face is

> evermore unseen
> And fixt upon the far sea-line.

And this view is, at any rate, not palpably unreasonable; since I shall have to admit that there is not on the chief questions of Philosophy, as I shall presently define it, any such *consensus of experts* as we find on questions of geometry, physics, botany.

general knowledge, each concerned with some part or aspect of the knowable world. This renders it in accordance with usage to follow Spencer in appropriating the term Philosophy to a study which, though in a manner *comprehensive* of all particular sciences, is not identical with any of them or even with the aggregate of them. Accordingly I shall regard Philosophy as 'in propriety' or 'by pre-eminence' aiming at such knowledge as is attainable by man of the *whole* of the apparently changing universe of things, as contrasted with the sciences which aim at general knowledge of particular kinds or elements or qualities of things and events, more or less separated off from other kinds or elements. But I allow also a wider and a looser use of 'Philosophy' and 'philosophical' as applied relatively to studies that are concerned with notions, principles, and methods that have a higher degree of generality than those of most special sciences, and thus find their application in several special sciences which in this way are connected into one system of knowledge.

The differences of philosophical schools are so great and fundamental that it would seem to be only by a polite fiction that a philosopher of one school allows a philosopher of another school to possess philosophical knowledge on the subjects that he treats: and the politeness that consents to this fiction is not universal —as it would be easy to show by quotations from very recent treatises. Candour compels me to own that philosophical knowledge, admitted to be such, is not to be obtained by following these lectures, as mathematical knowledge, *e.g.*, might be obtained by following the lectures of my mathematical colleagues.

We may note, however, that this objection does not apply to Natural Philosophy. If the Natural Philosopher is still pursuing, we all agree that he is not hunting with an empty bag. To this consideration I shall return, as it will help us to the definition that we are seeking. Meanwhile with regard to Philosophy, in the wider sense in which the term is commonly used without qualification, we may say that, even taking it merely as a pursuit, it is certainly a pursuit of knowledge: and we may call this knowledge 'philosophical,' without deciding how far it has yet been attained, and we may try to define what it would be if we had it, what questions it would answer.

From this point of view, then, let us return to examine further the relation of philosophical knowledge to the knowledge that we call scientific. It will be convenient to begin by getting a definition of Science. In the first place scientific knowledge is

THE SCOPE OF PHILOSOPHY

clearly systematic knowledge, or knowledge arranged and grasped in a certain order; a number of cognitions of particular facts, however accurately observed, do not constitute science so long as they remain loose and unconnected. Still knowledge may be systematised otherwise than in Science: thus History systematises our knowledge of past events by arranging them in order of time, and Geography systematises our knowledge of states, cities, rivers, mountains, etc. by giving a connected view of their positions on the surface of the globe. But neither of these arrangements is as such scientific, though scientific method may be required to work it out with accuracy and completeness. Shall we say then that Science systematises by ascertaining the causal relations of facts; that scientific knowledge is "knowledge of effects as dependent on their causes."[1] This is largely true; still it seems too narrow a conception for the ordinary denotation of the term. 'Science,' as ordinarily used, is applied to the abstract studies of relations of quantity which we class together as pure mathematics, where causation is altogether ignored: it is applied also to such studies as Botany and Zoology, where the investigation of causes, though it certainly forms a part of these studies, is not the sole ground of their claim to be called 'sciences.' It is, partly at least, as systematising the matter studied, by arranging objects according to relations of resemblance, that Botany and Zoology have been regarded as scientific. They have been called Sciences of Classification, and

[1] Hamilton, *Metaphysics*, vol. i. p. 58.

it was *primarily* as classificatory that they assumed the character of sciences: though all would agree that they reach a higher stage of development, so far as they become Sciences of Causation also.

To get a definition of Science applicable to all the instances named we must, I think, take the characteristic of 'generality' as the essential distinction between scientific knowledge and merely 'historical' knowledge of particular facts. The mathematical sciences deal with objects essentially general; the study of causes is a study of general laws or uniformities,—for a cause is a kind of thing which tends *generally*, and not merely in one particular case, to be followed by the kind of thing which we call its effect. The classificatory sciences are concerned, as their name imports, with classes—'genera' and 'species'—or general types. It is true that we largely regard knowledge of particular facts—*e.g.* of a new planet—as scientific knowledge; but only, I think, in view of its relation to general knowledge. Thus an uninstructed person might conceivably discover a new planet by accidentally looking through a telescope at the right time; but this observation would be unscientific, though of great value to science.

Now if we give this extended meaning to 'Science,' we see at once that some of the studies so called have no claim to be philosophical: we should not think of calling a Geometer or a Botanist—as such—a philosopher. But the case is different, as we saw, with Physics; and an examination of the difference seems likely to help us in our search for a definition of Philosophy which shall be as far as possible consistent with the common usage of the term.

Why does the Physicist claim to be a Philosopher? I think, because the great interest of his study is bound up with the belief that all the phenomena he investigates—however externally diverse their character—will be found explicable by the same system of dynamical principles, the same fundamental laws of matter and motion: a belief which has a solid foundation in the great—though as yet very imperfect—success that has even now been realised in working out this explanation in different departments. For example, considering the great *reach* of the Law of Gravitation, it seems to me in this wider sense to some extent legitimate that the Newtonian discovery should be called 'philosophical'; and again, that 'Theoretical Mechanics' be called 'Natural Philosophy.' To call it simply 'Philosophy' is, however, misleading, as that drops out of sight the essential aim of philosophy at explaining the *whole* of things; except so far as Theoretical Mechanics does claim to explain mind and its phenomena as well as matter, and refusing to recognise any other kind of existence than matter thus becomes Materialistic Philosophy according to the stricter definition of the term.[1]

[1] Of the untenability of Materialism I shall speak hereafter. My object now is only to point out that any thinker who holds that matter is the only reality, is according to my view *consistent*, and from his own point of view *right* in regarding the study of the most general laws of matter in motion, which used to be commonly called 'Natural Philosophy,' as being strictly Philosophy.

But if we investigate empirically the phenomena of Light, Heat, Sound, and Electricity, we find great diversity in the laws or uniformities which are ascertained by empirical observation and generalisation: *e.g.* the phenomena of the reflection and refraction of Light, of dispersion and colour, have not *primâ facie* any affinity with the phenomena of electrical attraction and repulsion, conduction and insulation. And I think it would be admitted that so far as an investigator aims at verifying or enlarging our knowledge of the special phenomena of Light or Electricity, it is 'Physical Science' rather than 'Natural Philosophy' that he is pursuing. It is only so far as he aims at systematising all these special laws as different applications of the general laws of matter in motion that he has a claim to the title of philosopher.

I regard 'Philosophy' then,—if the term is used without qualification—as the study which 'takes all knowledge for its province.' To such a study the human mind would be palpably incompetent if it attempted to deal with all the facts: it therefore selects the most important. Thus if we conceive the sciences as sets of connected knowledge, and imagine them as rising from the particular to the general, we may consider these sets in their turn as connected by Philosophy at the higher end. Philosophy, therefore, deals not with the whole matter of any science, but with the most important of its special notions, its fundamental principles, its distinctive method, its main conclusions. Philosophy examines

THE SCOPE OF PHILOSOPHY

these with the view of co-ordinating them with the fundamental notions and principles, methods and conclusions of other sciences. It may be called in this sense 'scientia scientiarum.'

The important distinction is that the Sciences concentrate attention on particular parts or aspects of the knowable world, abstracting from the rest; while it is, in contrast, the essential characteristic of Philosophy that it aims at putting together the parts of knowledge thus attained into a systematic whole; so that all methods of attaining truth may be grasped as parts of one method; and all the conclusions attained may be presented, so far as possible, as harmonious and consistent.

Perhaps some devotee of a special science may ask, "Is it worth while to do this till we have gone further in our knowledge of the parts?"

To this there is more than one answer. The most important answer I will give more fully later. Here I will say that in fact we cannot help doing it somehow. We grow up with ideas of the whole, which are continually modified as our knowledge extends: and no student of any special science ever acquiesces in having no idea of the relation of his part of knowledge to the rest. He may avoid philosophy in the sense of avoiding the attempt to make his conception of the universe as clear, precise, and systematic as possible, but that only means that he will be content with a vague, obscure, and altogether inadequate conception.

In fact, when a writer speaks of another's arguments as 'unphilosophical,' he often seems to mean no more than that he profoundly disagrees with him. It would, however, be a pity to allow the word to be used in this sense: and perhaps the different schools would agree that there is an instructed and an uninstructed way of reasoning on behalf of what each school regards as sound conclusions; the characteristic of an instructed way of reasoning being that it shows an adequate knowledge of the arguments used on the other side, some apprehension of their force, and that it endeavours either to meet or to avoid those arguments. Philosophical knowledge in this sense—on points on which experts are disagreed—would be knowledge of the confusions of thought to which the human intellect is liable when it begins to speculate on the questions of Philosophy: knowledge how to state these questions so as to avoid to some extent confusions of thought: and knowledge of considerations that have some force, though not necessarily decisive force, for or against conclusions on disputed questions of Philosophy. And if Philosophy is regarded as a subject of academic teaching and study, this, I conceive, is the kind of knowledge which the teacher ought mainly to seek to convey, on subjects of controversy.

But it is evident that this acquaintance with arguments is not the kind of knowledge at which Philosophy *aims*, although it may be all the knowledge for which a consensus of experts can be claimed at present. So long as this is so, the notion of philosophy being a *pursuit* rather than a system of knowledge will maintain itself, as it has maintained itself throughout two thousand years in which dogmatic systems have succeeded each other. This lack of a 'consensus of experts' as to the method and main conclusions of Philosophy, is, I fear, strong evidence that study of it is still—after so many centuries—in a rudimentary condition as compared with the more special studies of the branches of systematised knowledge that we call Sciences.

It ought to be the aim of all earnest students of Philosophy to remedy this defect: but no one can hope to remove suddenly and quickly so ancient and inveterate a deficiency. He can only hope to contribute somewhat towards its removal: and one way in which I hope to contribute to it in the present lectures is by fixing attention on the *questions* of Philosophy—since I hope it may be easier to come to approximate agreement when we try to define questions rather than answers: the knowledge we *want* rather than the knowledge we think we have got.

So far there is a broad and general agreement between my view and that given by Mr. Herbert Spencer in his chapter on 'Philosophy defined.' He says, 'The truths of Philosophy bear the same relation to the highest scientific truths, that each of these bears to lower scientific truths. As each widest generalisation of science comprehends and consolidates the narrower generalisations of its own division; so the generalisations of Philosophy comprehend and consolidate the widest generalisations of Science.'[1]

But I think this statement requires qualifying and

[1] *First Principles*, § 37.

supplementing in important respects. In proceeding to give the required qualifications and additions, it may be well to begin by answering an objection that may be taken—especially by a student of Metaphysics —to the whole view of Philosophy which Mr. Spencer holds and with which I agree so far as it is positive. It may be said :—"Any Science is concerned only with the *phenomenal*, can only claim to impart knowledge of *phenomena* to those who study it : well then, if you merely put the sciences and their results together, however successfully you combine and co-ordinate them you still have only phenomenal knowledge. Now the knowledge which Philosophy aims at is essentially different in kind from merely phenomenal knowledge : it is knowledge of the Realities behind or underlying phenomena. It therefore not only contemplates the Universe from a point of view different from that of any particular science, it contemplates an aspect entirely different from that contemplated by all sciences taken together."

It is the more important for me to notice this objection, because Mr. Spencer, with whom I am agreeing so far as my definition has yet gone, has already given it an answer with which I cannot agree. In the first five chapters of his treatise on *First Principles* he has proved to his own satisfaction that "the reality underlying appearances is totally and for ever inconceivable by us," and that, consequently, "the Philosophy which proposes to formulate Being as distinguished from appearance" is to be "repudiated as impossible." This is the doctrine which it is

THE SCOPE OF PHILOSOPHY

common and convenient to distinguish as 'Agnosticism.' By it, as Spencer admits, Philosophy is "shut out from much of the domain supposed to belong to it"; and the domain that is left—the laws of coexistence and sequence of phenomena—is, he says, "occupied by the sciences": so that it only remains for Philosophy to "consolidate the generalisation of science." Well, this view, it will be seen, is simple and coherent: but I cannot accept it.

On the one hand, I cannot admit—because I do not find that Science can admit—that Science is not concerned with Reality, but only with appearance: on the other hand, I cannot but admit that the Universe as a whole has or may have characteristics other than those with which the Sciences, especially at any rate the Sciences recognised by Spencer, are concerned, and therefore that knowledge is possible with regard to it other than that attained by the consolidation of these Sciences. But even if I were as Agnostic as Mr. Spencer professes to be—I shall hereafter try to show that he is not altogether as Agnostic as he seems—I should not import my Agnosticism into a definition of the Scope of Philosophy. For my aim is to give a definition which all schools may accept: and my plan of attaining this is, as I have said, to define the scope of Philosophy by ascertaining the questions which it asks, rather than the right answer to these questions. Now when it is once recognised that there is a Reality underlying or behind the Appearances of which the Sciences study the laws, it is certain that the desire of knowledge which leads men to philosophy will include the desire of knowing what can be known about this Reality : the question as to its fundamental nature and its relation [to Appearances] cannot then be excluded from the scope of Philosophy even if the question is to receive a negative answer. Indeed on this point I should appeal to Mr. Spencer's practice against his formal definition : because, as I said, this is the main question that he is discussing in the first five chapters of his *First Principles.*

On the other hand, to exclude the phenomena with which the Sciences are concerned from the scope of Philosophy, as some metaphysicians seem disposed to do, appears to me no less unwarrantable. For such phenomena—however much we may contrast the phenomenal with the real in a narrow sense—must be admitted to be a part of the universe of fact, and therefore a part of Reality in a wide sense. This is true even of the appearances that we commonly regard as palpably unreal. Suppose a man tells me that he saw a ghost yesterday afternoon at 5. P.M. : however convinced I am that it was a mere subjective hallucination, the apparition is none the less a real fact in the history of the mental experience of my informant. And it is of course obvious that reality of a sort must be held to belong to the world of colour and the world of sound which are in a manner common to normal human beings; and still more to the permanent material world about which Physical Science has sought and obtained knowledge. The question cannot be whether these so-called phenomena are or have been real, but what kind of reality belongs or has belonged to them.

I exclude, then, from the scope of Philosophy neither phenomena nor 'onta' or realities: and therefore, instead of Spencer's statement that Philosophy aims at generalisations which 'comprehend and consolidate the widest generalisations of Science,' it seems to me better to say that whereas in the study of any science we aim at knowing a *part* of the knowable world, contemplated in abstraction from the rest, as philosophers we aim at knowledge of the whole: and therefore at knowledge of the underlying reality, until Mr. Spencer convinces us that it is unknowable—and even then we want to know exactly how he knows it to be unknowable.

§ 3. At the same time I should like to keep Mr. Spencer's phrase 'completely unified knowledge': as it expresses the difference between the mere knowledge of a number of sciences, and a really philosophical grasp of the whole body of knowledge contained in these sciences taken together. And this leads me to note a deficiency which I seem to find in Mr. Spencer's conception of the unifying function of Philosophy. In the first of the phrases just quoted—' comprehend and consolidate the widest generalisation of science'—too exclusive a stress seems to be laid on relations of identity or resemblance, relations of difference being too much ignored. No doubt our knowledge is in some degree 'unified' so far as particular truths, hitherto held separately, are comprehended in a wider generalisation: but the differences of the particular truths will still remain, and unless the wider generalisation enables us to comprehend these differences, our knowledge will not be *completely* unified. The complete unification at which Philosophy aims must enable us to view every portion of knowledge—and every object known—as a part of a coherent whole : and in comprehending the relation of diverse parts of a whole to the whole, and to each other, systematic difference — difference essentially belonging to the nature of the whole—is as important a feature as resemblance.

This statement is perhaps hardly clear without illustration. What, it may be asked, is exactly meant by comprehending differences as 'rational' and 'systematic' and 'following from the nature of the whole'? The best way to make this clear will be to take some case in which sciences have been—as Mr. Spencer says —'unified' by the comprehension of narrower in wider generalisations. I will take the most famous case, the identification, worked out mathematically by Newton, of the fundamental laws of terrestrial with the fundamental laws of celestial motion. When men began to observe and reflect on physical phenomena, the movements of falling bodies to the earth seemed as unlike as possible to the movements of the starry heavens : the former moved in a straight line, and the latter—apart from the problem presented by the planets—were, it seemed, circular and uniform. In each case the true view of the matter was impeded by erroneous inferences from observation—in the case of terrestrial motion by the erroneous idea that heavy

THE SCOPE OF PHILOSOPHY

bodies fall quicker than light bodies, and in the case of celestial motions by the simple and inevitable geocentric hypothesis.

Well, we all know vaguely how the erroneous view of terrestrial motions was cleared away—chiefly by Galileo ; and the heliocentric substituted for the geocentric hypothesis — chiefly through the work of Copernicus—and how the marvellous industry and genius of Kepler working on the observations of Tycho Brahe had ascertained the empirical laws of the movements of planets round the sun—*i.e.* that they moved not in circles but in ellipses with the sun in one focus, and that each moved at such a rate as to describe equal areas of the orbit in equal times. When the knowledge of the two kinds of motion had come to this point, matters were ripe for the great identification which comprehended planetary motions as a case of the operation of the law of universal gravitation.

But, you will observe, this identification or unification did not merely point out the similarity between the two kinds of motion, but it at the same time explained the differences — explained, that is, why bodies fall to the earth approximately in a straight line, while planets go round the sun in ellipses : these *prima facie* diverse kinds of motion being both viewed as different applications of the same general laws of matter in motion.

Now take, by contrast, Mr. Spencer's great generalisation—the doctrine of Evolution. Mr. Spencer claims to comprehend the chief laws of the changes through which the world of inorganic matter has passed in time, the laws of the world of organic life, and the laws of mental development, by comprehending them under the same great law of Evolution or 'progress from indefinite, incoherent homogeneity to definite, coherent heterogeneity.' I shall have occasion to criticise this doctrine later on: but what I now wish to point out is that however completely we may grant that certain resemblances have been made out between (1) the laws of change in inorganic and organic matter and (2) the laws of change and development of mind, the resemblance does not in the least help us to explain the differences between the world of living things and the inorganic world. The differences between mind and matter still remain unexplained by the generalisation, and present unsolved problems for philosophy, just as obstinate and perplexing, *after* we have admitted the evolutional doctrine, as they were before.

I say this, not because I do not think Spencer's doctrine, so far as true, of philosophical importance; but because he seems to me in any case to over-estimate the contribution made by it to the solution of the problems of philosophy. This over-estimate accords with and conveniently illustrates the defect in his general definition of philosophy that I have been trying to explain.

LECTURE II

THE SCOPE OF PHILOSOPHY (*continued*)

§ 1. So far, though I have suggested an important modification of Mr. Spencer's description of the work of Philosophy, I have accepted his view of the matter on which Philosophy works: that is, I have taken this to consist of the partially systematised aggregates of knowledge which we call the sciences, regarding it as the business of philosophy to systematise these more completely. But I must now announce and explain an important divergence from his view on this latter point. 'Science' as the term is used by Mr. Spencer —and by me—means exclusively what is sometimes distinguished as 'Positive Science.' That is, according to Mr. Spencer, it "concerns itself with the co-existences and sequences among phenomena." I have objected to this mode of speaking, since by 'phenomenon' we mean, or may mean, 'appearance' as contrasted with 'reality': and certainly the students of science generally would not admit that they have no knowledge of real existence. But Mr. Spencer cannot mean to affirm this: the philosopher of Evolution cannot be supposed to hold that the great process of development through time of the inorganic world, the world of organic life, and human society—which he has described in several volumes—is not a real process; that the series of changes grasped and systematically presented by the 'Synthetic Philosophy' is not a real succession of real events. I take him to mean that Science cannot thoroughly comprehend what really exists: that behind the varied complex of existences and changes with which the sciences deal there is hidden an unknowable and inscrutable 'Ultimate Reality.' This view I reserve for later discussion; meanwhile I think that, without material disagreement with Mr. Spencer, we may say that the knowledge at which the sciences aim, and which they claim to have partially attained, is knowledge of what exists or has existed or will exist.

If so, it seems clear that the matter presented by Science so defined cannot be regarded as the whole of the matter on which Philosophy has to work. For Philosophy must deal with the principles and methods of rationally determining 'what ought to be,' as distinct from the principles and methods of ascertaining what is, has been, and will be. The current use of the terms 'Moral' and 'Political' Philosophy clearly implies this department of the work of Philosophy. We cannot say that there is no such thing as Moral or Political Philosophy, without violent divergence from common thought and common usage of terms: and on the other hand we cannot say that Moral or Political Philosophy has for its business the co-ordination of the co-existences and sequences of phenomena, without neglecting the fundamental distinction between 'what ought to be' and what actually is or appears. We must therefore, I think, give a wider scope to the term 'Philosophy' than we have hitherto given, and regard it as including in the range of its 'unifying' function not only the systems of knowledge commonly called 'sciences' or 'positive sciences,' but also the systems of knowledge or reasoned thought distinguished as Ethics, Politics, and Jurisprudence.

It would, of course, be absurd to suggest that Mr. Spencer—the author of two volumes on the 'Principles of Ethics,' which are labelled on the back 'Synthetic Philosophy'—could possibly have designed to exclude the subject-matter of Ethics from the scope of Philosophy. The question is on what terms he is willing to admit it. The full discussion of this question will naturally come when we study his system in detail. But I may here say briefly that though in one passage he speaks of Ethics as a "science dealing with the conduct of associated human beings," it is not easy to gather from his language how far he really supposes himself to treat scientifically the whole subject as he conceives it— not merely the method of ascertaining the *means* to what he regards as the ultimate end of right conduct, but the method of establishing the *end and defining that with adequate clearness and precision*. I conjecture that he does regard this as included in his scientific treatment, though I confess I have no doubt in my own mind that he does not treat this part of the subject by any method that seems even to claim scientific character. But—whatever method we adopt—it certainly seems to me that the discussion of the ultimate end of right conduct is *not* concerned with 'the co-existences and sequences of phenomena.'

It will be observed that in my statements about Ethics and Politics I leave the method undefined, and therefore do not enter into the question how far it is scientific. I wish to have a comprehensive definition suitable for all schools, Intuitional as well as Utilitarian and Evolutional. At the same time, from the neutral point of view that I adopt in my search for a definition, it is important to note that there is a school of philosophers which would refuse to recognise the distinction between what is and what ought to be. Regarding Ethics, etc., as a 'descriptive, not a normative' science, they consider it the business of Ethics to study actual conduct as determined by certain laws obtaining in the social organism.

Perhaps, just as we recognise a Materialistic Philosophy, which regards Theoretical Mechanics as explaining the whole universe of the knowable, so we may recognise a Naturalistic or Positive Philosophy which, going beyond Materialism by including subjective Psychology, still refuses to allow systematic knowledge of what ought to be as such—distinguished from Positive Science as not concerned except indirectly with what is, has been, and will be—to form a part of the whole body of knowledge which it is the business of Philosophy to unify.

I quite admit that a thinker who recognises no

object of knowledge except what exists, has existed, or will exist in time, may properly accept Spencer's definition of Philosophy : and it is perhaps convenient to label this manner of thought as 'Naturalistic' or 'Positive' Philosophy. But I do not think it clear that a thinker of this type will regard Ethics as a positive Science : but rather, perhaps, as an Art based on Biology, Psychology, and Sociology.

§ 2. I have spoken of Ethics, Politics, and Jurisprudence. The last mentioned is clearly distinguished in ordinary thought from Philosophy. There are, no doubt, philosophical jurists; but all jurists are not as such philosophers : it is recognised that a man may have a sound knowledge of law—even of the conceptions and rules of law in general, as distinct from the law of a particular state—without being at all a philosopher. The distinction between Ethics or Politics and Philosophy is not so clear : still I think that some distinction is vaguely made in ordinary thought, and might with advantage be made somewhat more explicit. It is vaguely recognised that it is the business of *Ethics* to supply an answer to questions as to details of duty or right conduct—so far as they are questions which it is held legitimate, and not idle, to ask—but that this is not the business of Moral or Ethical *Philosophy*, which is primarily concerned with the general principles and methods of moral reasoning, and only with details of conduct so far as the discussion of them affords instructive examples of general principles and method. It is commonly felt that an attempt to work out a complete system of duties would inevitably lead us out of Philosophy into Casuistry: and that whether Casuistry is a good thing or a bad thing, it certainly is not Philosophy.

A similar distinction may, I think, be applied to Politics:—accordingly when I had to select a title for a bulky volume in which I have attempted to treat systematically the chief questions for which the statesman has to find answers, I called the book 'Elements of Politics,' not 'Political Philosophy' or 'Political Science.' I did not call it Political Philosophy, since it aims at determining the rules for governmental action, and for the construction of governmental organs with more fulness of detail than it belongs to Philosophy to do: nor, again, did I call it Political Science, since it is primarily concerned with polity as it ought to be, and not with polities as they are, have been, and—so far as we can foresee—will be.

I think, then, that we have to recognise it as part of the business of Philosophy, to 'unify' the principles and methods of reasoning directed to practical conclusions, which we call 'political' when they refer to the constitution and action of government, and 'ethical' when they refer to private conduct. We may call this part or function of Philosophy 'practical,' as distinct from the Philosophy that seeks to unify those sciences, which we may suitably call 'theoretical' or 'positive,'—according as we wish to imply that the objects of scientific knowledge are *real* or merely *phenomenal*. Taking science as conversant with real existence, I shall provisionally use the term 'theoretical.'

I may point out that by taking the notion of Practical Philosophy to include the study of the principles and methods of Ethics and Politics, we may postpone the question which of these is prior to the other. This is a question on both sides of which there are important arguments. On the one hand it is urged that man is essentially a 'political animal' —a member of a State or governed society, whose manner of life is necessarily determined by the position that he holds in his society: and that, as Aristotle says, the attainment of wellbeing for the State is a higher and more comprehensive end than the attainment of wellbeing for a single individual. On the other hand it may be said that any man as a rational being has relations to the Universe, and to the ordering Reason manifested by the Universe, which are prior to, and more fundamental than his relation to the political society of which he happens to be a member—especially as he is usually at perfect liberty to change it.

I shall enter further into these arguments when I come to the fuller discussion of Practical Philosophy [see Prefatory Note]. Here I only throw out this question as an illustration of the business that Practical Philosophy has to do: it has to try to establish an intelligible relation between the sphere of Ethics and the sphere of Politics. For the present, however, I take Practical Philosophy to include the study of the fundamental principles of Ethics and Politics, and therefore to be at least equivalent to what is commonly spoken of as a Moral and Political Philosophy. As such it must be a supreme architectonic study of ultimate ends, of the principles of what ought to be. So taken it seems to hold a position in reference to *Arts* in general, somewhat similar [1] to that which Theoretical Philosophy holds with reference to Sciences in general.

In speaking of Arts I mean—using the term in its widest sense—all departments of human activity, carried on systematically with reasoned adaptation of means to ends, for the attainment of some particular end, other than the knowledge applied in the Art. I thus include not merely handicrafts and what are distinguished as 'Fine Arts,' but also such professions as Medicine and Strategy. When we contemplate human life as a whole and consider the place that any one Art ought to hold in it, we see at once that some Arts are obviously subordinate to others, and these again to others still higher and more comprehensive: but when we try to make the systematisation of Arts and Ends complete, doubts and difficulties are apt to present themselves for the solution of which we require such a study as I have called Practical Philosophy.

The subordinate position of such Arts as aim at

[1] I ought to point out that the similarity is not very close. The systematisation of the Arts by Practical Philosophy relates primarily and mainly, as we have seen, to the *ends* of the Arts. For the reasoned adaptation of means to ends which constitutes the greater part of any Art, so far as its method is formulated and expressed, so that it is capable of being learnt from books—this is mainly scientific reasoning taken from one or more sciences, and arranged and combined, with a view to the special purposes of the Art. I think—as I have already said—that Ethics, from the point of view of those whom we have agreed to call Naturalistic or Positive Philosophers, is likely to turn out rather an Art that combines scientific reasonings from Biology, Physiology, Psychology, and Sociology than strictly a branch of science.

the production of 'utilities fixed in material objects' —as economists say—or such immaterial utilities as conveyance, communication, victory in war, etc.,— is usually manifest. Any such Art aims at a result which is clearly only desirable as a means to some further end, the desirability of which it does not belong to this Art to investigate. It is the business of the commander-in-chief to beat the enemy: it is not his business to determine whether war ought to be begun; that is admittedly the business of the Statesman. But when we ask on what principles the statesman is to determine it—*e.g.* whether his ultimate end is to be the preservation or wellbeing of his own state, or the wellbeing or happiness of humanity at large—we raise questions on which the practical maxims of statesmen are apt to disagree with the prescriptions of ordinary morality: so that we seem to require Practical Philosophy to settle the conflict.

Again, there are cases where the End aimed at in an Art is not clearly a means to some further end, but claims to be good in itself without reference to anything beyond—*e.g.* some would affirm this of the Beauty at which the Fine Arts aim. But at any rate this Beauty is only one element and not the whole of human good: the problem therefore is still left of comparing and co-ordinating it with other elements of good. Hence we may say generally of all arts, that, regarded as departments of rational action, they are naturally subordinate to and systematised by a theory of rational action as a whole — whether of human beings individually or of communities of human beings—such as Practical Philosophy seeks to work out.

§ 3. We have thus arrived at the conception of Practical Philosophy as a study distinct from and in a manner parallel to Philosophy as conceived by Mr. Spencer. But in insisting on the recognition of the two departments of Philosophy as fundamental and important, I do not wish to imply that there is an absolute separation between them : and that there are in reality two quite separate studies, one systematising the different sciences, and the other systematising the different ends of human action and the different sets of rules for practice, or ideals of what ought to be. On the contrary, I wish to emphasise, as the final and most important task of Philosophy, the problem of co-ordinating these two divisions of its subject-matter, and connecting fact and ideal in some rational and satisfactory manner. The problem, however, must be recognised as a very difficult one. For its solution should enable us to answer the question 'How comes it that what ought to be is not and yet ought to be?': or, negatively, 'Whence comes the existence of what ought not to be?' And any one who knows anything of the history of human thought may well despair of attaining a satisfactory answer to this question ;—unless he holds firmly to the conviction that such despair, at any rate, is one of the things that ought not to be.[1]

We may then provisionally recognise as distinct,

[1] See Appendix at the end of this lecture.

Theoretical Philosophy, aiming at a systematisation of Sciences, and Practical Philosophy, aiming at a complete systematisation of Arts, including Ethics and Politics. We must not, however, make the distinction between art and science too profound. Firstly, it is to be noted that Arts in the aggregate and Sciences in the aggregate do not consist respectively of entirely different knowledge, but, as we have just seen, of the same knowledge arranged or viewed differently—so far at least as the rules of Art are based on real knowledge.[1] Secondly, as Mr. Spencer observes,[2] "the Sciences become Arts to one another": *i.e.* some kinds of systematised general knowledge are clearly useful, and used as a means to the attainment of other knowledge. Further, all Sciences, even if not pursued for any ulterior end, may be regarded from a point of view which assimilates them to Arts. For the study of any science is a species of rational activity pursued for an end—the attainment of a particular kind of knowledge; and the question of the value and relative importance of this knowledge is a reasonable question to ask: and if it is a reasonable question to ask, it obviously belongs to Practical Philosophy to answer it, just as it belongs to Practical Philosophy to answer the corresponding question with regard to any Art.

Indeed, from this point of view Theoretical Philosophy itself seems subordinate to Practical Philosophy. For the pursuit of knowledge of the

---

[1] Cf. Mill's *Examination of Hamilton*, ch. xx.

[2] *Essays*, "Genesis of Science," 1868, vol. i. p. 189.

whole knowable universe may, no less than the study of any special science, be regarded as a particular kind of rational activity, which has to be compared and co-ordinated with other modes of human life and action : from this point of view we consider how far such knowledge is an end in itself and how far a means to some further end, and how large a place the pursuit of it ought to occupy in the right organisation of human existence,—all which questions manifestly come within the scope assigned to Practical Philosophy.

I may illustrate this by answering the objection made by Sir W. Hamilton [1] to the distinction which I have adopted between Theoretical Philosophy and Practical Philosophy. He says that all Philosophy is in a sense theoretical, because it is cognitive, while again all Philosophy is in a sense practical, because its end is the 'practical energy' exercised in the process of cognition. I answer by agreeing that in my conception of Practical Philosophy, I extend the notion of Practice, beyond what is customary, to include all forms of human activity—as Hamilton himself does in speaking of practical energy exercised in cognition. And thus Theoretical Philosophy is no doubt in a sense practical, because it is a department of human activity, but in this aspect it is not to be *identified* with Practical Philosophy, but to be subordinated to it.

The question : What is the *utility* of (Theoretical) Philosophy, what is the ultimate end for which we

[1] *Lectures on Metaphysics*, vol. i. p. 113.

ought to philosophise? is one that *relates* to Theoretical Philosophy: but it is one that belongs to Practical Philosophy to deal with. Knowledge of the right end or ends of rational action, of the manner in which different ends are to be harmonised, or subordinated one to another, is not knowledge which can be obtained by any of the positive Sciences concerned with the 'co-existences and sequences of phenomena,' or even by Philosophy regarded merely as co-ordinating these sciences: questions of ends are indeed philosophical questions: but they are questions which it belongs to *Practical* Philosophy or Philosophy in its practical aspect to answer.

On the other hand, from another point of view Practical Philosophy seems to be subordinate to Theoretical. Theoretical Philosophy, as above distinguished, deals with what is, not with what ought to be. But there is a sense in which what ought to be is, or we could not reason or talk about it. The thing itself which ought to be does not *as such* exist. It may actually exist or it may not; but the question whether it exists or not does not primarily concern Practical Philosophy. Secondarily, however, it does; because actuality proves possibility, and it is useless and therefore wrong to spend labour in efforts to realise the impossible. But what Practical Philosophy is primarily concerned with is desirability and possibility, not actuality: whether what ought to be exists or not, the *idea* or *thought* of it exists in human minds, so far as we can talk of it at all. The ideal is actual in idea. Hence all the propositions of

Practical Philosophy regarded as human thoughts or judgments or beliefs are seen to be parts of that sphere of cognisable existence with which Theoretical Philosophy is concerned.[1]

From this point of view we may co-ordinate the positive sciences, regarded as systems of reasoned thoughts or judgments, with the systems of practical reasonings that constitute the different arts—including Ethics and Politics—so far as the rules of Art are reasoned rules; and may consider that the aim of Philosophy, in its widest sense, is to comprehend all rational human thought—whether it relates to 'what is' or to 'what ought to be'—as one coherent whole. Observe an important change in our point of view. We began by regarding the whole of which Philosophy seeks knowledge as a whole of things; we are now led to contemplate it as a whole of thought. Theoretical Philosophy thus viewed—and made to include Practical Philosophy as subordinate—seems to become a study of the thoughts or beliefs of the

---

[1] To illustrate the kind of relations that, from this point of view, may be seen to exist between positive Sciences on the one hand, and studies that deal with what ought to be, I may refer to the comparison which many thinkers have held it important to make between the fundamental notions and principles of Ethics, and the fundamental notions and principles of Geometry.

Though Geometry is concerned with the relations of co-existence among things or phenomena which are objects of sense-perception, and Ethics with the determination of what ought to be, still many thinkers from earliest to latest times have discerned profound affinity between the fundamental notions of the two. *E.g.* when we are told that Pythagoras held that the essence of Justice was a square number, the statement appears fantastic and absurd. But when Mr. Spencer points out (*Essays*, 'Genesis,' p. 51) that the notion of 'Equality' which is fundamental in mathematics also underlies morals and is an essential element of the conception of Justice, we cannot but admit that the comparison may be instructive.

human mind, with a view to their complete systematisation.

§ 4. This leads me to the consideration of a view of the meaning and scope of Philosophy which I have so far left on one side, the view, namely, that the 'Science of Mind' or 'of Man' is 'Philosophy Proper,' or the main part of it. I think it may be said that a generation ago this was the predominant opinion among English thinkers. In 1868 the foremost debate in English thought was between the philosophy of Sir W. Hamilton and that of J. S. Mill: and both these thinkers, in defining Philosophy, seem to take the view that I have just given. Thus Sir W. Hamilton says that "The science of mind . . . constitutes the principal and most important object of philosophy . . . constitutes in propriety, with its suite of dependent sciences, Philosophy itself": the 'dependent sciences' being, apparently, Logic, Ethics, Politics—"so far as it supposes a knowledge of man in his natural constitution"[1]—and also Æsthetics, and Theology. So again J. S. Mill—with more express recognition of the social aspect of human life—takes "the proper meaning of Philosophy to be . . . the scientific knowledge of Man, as an intellectual, moral, and social being."[2] And this view,—which seems to blend Philosophy indistinguishably with Psychology or Sociology or both—still survives among us: indeed it seems to be implied in the term 'Mental Philo-

[1] *Lectures on Metaphysics*, vol. i. pp. 62, 63.

[2] *Auguste Comte and Positivism*, p. 53. This passage, which represents Mill's mature view, clearly does not distinguish Philosophy from Psychology or Sociology.

sophy' which forms a part of the title of our new chair. On the other hand it appears difficult to reconcile with the view that the aim of Philosophy is to unify or systematise the sciences; since mind is commonly regarded as the subject of a special science, Psychology, having its special place in the classification of the sciences; and a younger special science, Sociology—whose claims are less generally admitted by its elders—takes as its special subject-matter man regarded as a social being. The conflict of conceptions thus presented seems to me deserving of careful consideration.[1]

Here I will only say that Psychology, viewed as a special science, has—by the admission of all but Materialists—a peculiar position among the sciences: it is at once peculiarly distinct from and peculiarly connected with all the rest. On the one hand, as Mr. Spencer says,[2] "under its subjective aspect, Psychology is a totally unique science, independent of, and antithetically opposed to, all other sciences whatever. The thoughts and feelings which constitute a consciousness . . . form an existence which has no place among the existences with which the rest of the sciences deal." On the other hand, however exclusively we may concentrate attention on Mind regarded as a particular kind of thing, distinct from

---

[1] My desire is to give a distinct meaning to each of the three terms: but a consideration of the relation of Philosophy to Sociology will carry us away from Metaphysics: whereas a consideration of the relation of Philosophy to Psychology will lead us to Metaphysics by a convenient road. Deferring Sociology, therefore, I shall treat of this latter relation in the next lecture.

[2] *Psychology*, vol. i. p. 140.

and 'without kinship with' the Matter with which the physical sciences are concerned, we soon find that among the most important of the phenomena of the particular human minds that we study—each one's own or another's—are Thoughts, Judgments, and Beliefs; and that we cannot study these without studying their objects. Hence — since everything that we know or believe to be, or to have been, and everything which we believe ought to be, not to speak of the still wider world which we regard as possible, has necessarily the characteristic of being thought about—it would seem that Psychology, however it may begin as a special science, inevitably broadens out into a study as comprehensive in its range as Philosophy, according to the widest view which we have been led to take of Philosophy. It may, indeed, be urged that the range of existence extends infinitely beyond the range of what is known —or in any way definitely thought by any finite mind—and it would be paradoxical to deny this. But it is evident that of existence as so extending, Philosophy cannot, any more than Psychology, have anything definite to say. The point at which definite thought ends, and indefinite and inadequate thought begins, is obviously the same for both studies.

We thus see that the matter of Philosophy is difficult to distinguish from the matter of Psychology. At the same time, I think it fundamentally important to distinguish the two studies as clearly as we can : and I propose to attempt this in the following lecture.

APPENDIX TO LECTURE II

RELATION OF PHILOSOPHY TO RELIGION

THE reference to the 'problem of Evil' (p. 30) leads me to a topic which finds no place in this lecture—the relation of Philosophy to Religion. The importance of this relation, and the prominence given to it in some attempts to define the Scope of Philosophy (*e.g.* Wundt's, and—in a negative way—Spencer's), render it desirable that I should give my reasons for the omission.

In the first place, I may say that it was not due to any desire to depreciate the importance of Theology or to leave it on one side. On the contrary, as I have tried to indicate, the fundamental question to which Theology gives an answer—as to the relation of what is to what ought to be—represents, in my view, "the final and most important task of philosophy." And the answer which Theology gives to this question—to whatever criticisms it may be legitimately open—must be admitted, in the view of the common sense of mankind, to 'hold the field.'

I have referred to this again in Lecture IV.,[1] and what is there said will partly explain why I have omitted any discussion of the relation of Philosophy to Religion in this lecture. As I there intimate, there are two essentially distinct methods of attaining the intellectual convictions which constitute the essential framework for the play of religious emotion and the exercise of religious worship. I distinguish these methods and their results as Rational and Revelational Theology.

As to Rational Theology, it seems to me that the questions with which it deals—questions relating to the One Universal and Eternal Mind, which we conceive God to be, and His relation to the physical world and to human minds—are *primâ facie* philosophical questions, according to my definition : *i.e.* they belong to the contemplation of the Universe as a whole. Rational Theology then cannot properly be placed on a par with the

[1] See below, p. 94.

special sciences, which deal separately—as has been said—with different parts or aspects of the knowable world. And again, it seems to me that these questions belong to that part or kind of philosophy commonly called Metaphysics : *i.e.* always supposing that in trying to answer them we rely simply on the exercise of the human reason, and do not seek guidance from Revelation.

An objection, however, may be made to this, which I admit to have much force. It may be urged that what I have said applies to the conception of God with which speculative and metaphysical reasonings have been mainly concerned ; to God conceived as the First Cause of the world; or to God as the Infinite and Perfect Being, contrasted with the finite and imperfect beings that we empirically know; or as the Absolute Reality in contrast with the relative realities of which alone we are alleged to have experience : but that it does not apply to God as the object of religious thought and worship. God, it may be said, as so contemplated, is thought of under a very different series or system of notions. He is thought of as having a Righteous Will, the content of which, so far as it relates to man, is partially apprehended by man under the form of rules of duty; He is thought of as standing to human beings in a relation fitly symbolised by the relation of a father to his children; He is thought of as source of aid and strength in the never-ending struggle with sin which forms an essential element of the higher moral life ; finally He is thought of as centre and sovereign of a spiritual kingdom of which human beings are or may be members. These and other cognate conceptions, it may be urged, constitute the real thought-element of the common religious consciousness of man in his highest stage of development; and not the metaphysical ideas of First Cause, Infinite and Absolute Being, etc. And these common religious ideas, it may be held, should be taken as expressing or symbolising the aspect of reality apprehended through the religious consciousness, just as our common system of physical ideas—our conception of the world as a coherent aggregate of extended things occupying and moving in space of three dimensions—expresses or symbolises the aspect of reality apprehended through the senses. On this view the system of religious ideas would occupy a more or less co-ordinate position with the Sciences, as a department of the whole body of partially systematised thought, which it is the task of the philosopher to reduce, if he can, to a consistent and coherent whole.

The view which I have tried briefly to express is one to which I have every desire to do full justice. My reason for not introducing it into a lecture on the 'scope of philosophy' was not that I denied the existence of this common element of religious thought; but that I was impressed with the difficulty either of separating it sufficiently from the historical element with which it is combined in current Revelational Theologies, or if I introduced it along with this historical element, of giving any statement of it that could at all claim to rank—in respect of consensus of experts—with the positive Sciences. I by no means say that there should not be made a serious effort to overcome this difficulty: but I think it must be made, in the first instance, by theologians.

LECTURE III

THE RELATION OF PHILOSOPHY TO PSYCHOLOGY

§ 1. In the present lecture I propose to examine the relation of Philosophy, viewed as the study of rational thought as a whole, to Psychology or the Science of Mind. A generation ago there was, as pointed out in the last lecture, a prevalent tendency to fuse the two studies into one, under the name of 'Mental Philosophy'; and no doubt Mind occupies a unique and central position in the known world, as that which knows or thinks of all that is known or thought of. At the same time we commonly consider minds and their states as only a part of the object of knowledge; we consider Mind a particular kind of thing, which along with the varieties of another kind of thing called Matter, makes up the world of empirically known fact. This is the view that we all take in ordinary thought and discourse, and accordingly I shall begin by assuming it; reserving for subsequent discussion the objections brought against it by Mentalists and Materialists respectively.

I have explained that my aim in trying to define the Scope of Philosophy is to obtain if possible a definition acceptable to all schools : and that, in order to attain this, I should concentrate attention on the questions which Philosophy asks, rather than the answers to be given to them—it being easier to get the opposing schools to agree about the questions than about the answers. Perhaps on hearing this some member of my audience—acquainted with metaphysical controversy—may have thought that the distinction would turn out illusory; and that the differences of the schools would necessarily come in, in the form of putting the fundamental questions; that, in short, if you allow a metaphysician to put his questions in his own way, he can always manage—if he knows his business—to put them so that you can hardly help giving the answers he wants.

I quite admit the difficulty : but I think that it is possible to be on one's guard against it, and specially easy to be on one's guard from my metaphysical standpoint—which is speaking broadly that of what has been called since Reid the Philosophy of Common Sense or Natural Dualism. For there is this advantage in putting questions from the point of view of Common Sense : that it is, in some degree, in the minds of us all, even of the metaphysicians whose conclusions are most opposed to it—such as the extreme Sensationalist or Idealist. It is the view with which we all start when we begin to philosophise, whatever metaphysical conclusions we may ultimately adopt (Materialist, Sensationalist, or Idealist): and therefore it will be a philosophical gain to bring it as clearly as we can before the full gaze of reflective attention, even though further consideration should lead us to abandon or modify it.

In saying this I do not mean to affirm—as some who have maintained Natural Dualism as a philosophical conclusion have affirmed — that Natural Dualism is involved in the *original* presentation of the objects of experience to the experiencing mind. That is a question to be reserved for subsequent discussion, on which I now express no opinion even provisionally. All I affirm is that we find it in our ordinary thought when we begin to reflect on it, nor can we by the utmost effort of memory recall a time when we did not implicitly hold it. If the belief in an external material world existing as we know it independently of our knowing it—so that our knowledge of it does not affect its existence—if this belief is the result of inference from data given originally as merely mental fact, this process of inference preceded the stage of conscious reflection. I ought further to explain that in speaking of Common Sense I do not mean entirely unscientific Common Sense, but the Common Sense of educated persons rectified by a general acquaintance with the results and methods of physical science. In the latter part of this course I shall have to go more fully into the extent and significance of this 'rectification' by science of the plain man's view of matter and mind: in this lecture I only assume it in a broad and general way.

I must repeat that I do not put forward Natural Dualism now dogmatically, but only provisionally. I am quite aware that there are serious difficulties when we try to make the view of Common Sense clear and consistent: and I do not wish to ignore them. But I think that considerable confusion arises from not trying to make it as clear as we can: especially since the distinction between Mind and Matter, which Natural Dualism takes as fundamental, must be recognised as important from any point of view. *E.g.* the difference between (1) my feelings and thoughts, and (2) what goes on in my brain when I feel and think, cannot be got rid of by saying that after all everything is consciousness: this I shall try to show later.

Let us then attempt, taking frankly this point of view, to distinguish as clearly as possible the task of Philosophy from that of Psychology. According to Common Sense or Natural Dualism, Mind—while occupying a unique position in the known world, as that which knows everything else and which therefore, as knowing subject, is at once connected and contrasted with all its known objects—is at the same time a particular thing alongside of other things: is an object or part of the object as well as the sole subject of knowledge.

Taking this view, then, we see that Mind may be considered either (1) in itself, abstracting as far as possible from Matter, or (2) in relation to Matter; and both Philosophy and Psychology must consider it in this latter relation, though primarily for different reasons: Philosophy because its task is to put all the sciences together into a systematic whole, Psychology because of the intimate connection between mental facts and nerve-processes. I propose accordingly to consider the relation between the two studies from both points of view successively.

§ 2. Philosophy, as we have seen, is concerned with knowledge and the reasoned thought that determines action so far as rational. These are mental facts, and as such a part of the subject-matter of Psychology; but *primâ facie* they are only a part. The minds empirically known to us not only think, but also have sensations; not only act in accordance with rational judgment or belief as to what is right or good, but also in conflict with such judgment or belief, under the influence of the feelings we call pleasures, pains, desires, and aversions. If the *only* function of the mind were to think, if the only phenomena it exhibited were thoughts, cognitions, judgments, beliefs, there would be more difficulty in distinguishing Psychology from that reflection or knowledge which —so far as pursued with the view of systematising knowledge—we have called Philosophy. So again, if the only other attribute of the mind were Rational Volition, or action for rational ends chosen as *per se* good or desirable, there would be a similar difficulty in distinguishing the part of Psychology dealing with the general principles of such volition from Practical Philosophy, which must include an exhaustive investigation of the ultimate ends or principles of Rational Volition, and of the processes of thought by which the right means to these ends are to be chosen.

But we have in Feeling[1] and Feeling-prompted

---

[1] I use the term Feeling in the older English meaning, in which it includes

volition a peculiar subject-matter for Psychology considered as a special science, which only comes within the scope of Philosophy as the subject-matter of any other science does :—*i.e.* in respect of its main outlines, the fundamental ideas applicable to it, the methods of investigating it, and the chief conclusions thereby attained. Or at any rate if Philosophy has any more special concern with Feelings and Feeling-prompted volitions than I have thus indicated, it is because their special connexion with Thoughts and Reasoned Purposes has caused some confusion between the two kinds of mental fact; and has led some thinkers to regard the Feelings which undoubtedly antecede and accompany cognition as the simple elements out of which knowledge and its object—the known world—are compounded. No doubt, so far as this view—which I shall consider presently—is held, the coincidence in subject-matter between .Philosophy and Psychology becomes more complete. It thus appears that the relation between Philosophy and Psychology will necessarily be somewhat different for different schools—as we have seen to be the case with the relation between Philosophy and Physics. Just as in the view of Materialists, who hold that everything knowable must be ultimately reducible to some complex kind or mode of matter in motion, Philosophy cannot be effectually and finally distinguished from Rational Physics, so far as its positive and constructive work is concerned;

what are commonly called sensations of colour and sound, as well as what are commonly called sensations of pleasure and pain.

so in the view of those who resolve everything knowable into feeling, or more widely, into the states of consciousness of particular minds, Philosophy cannot be effectually and finally distinguished from Psychology, except, again, on its negative side.[1]

Such Psychological Philosophy, however, is like Materialistic Philosophy, paradoxical: in the one we have Rational Physics endeavouring to swell itself out into a Theory of the Universe as a whole, and in the other we have the Science of Mind doing the same thing. In both we have a similar divergence, but in opposite directions, from the point of view of Common Sense or Natural Dualism. Returning now to this point of view, let us pass on to contemplate the admitted common ground of Philosophy and Psychology—Thoughts, Judgments, Beliefs. I shall try to show that there are important differences between the methods and aims of the two studies in treating this common subject-matter. These differences chiefly spring from or are connected with an essential characteristic of thoughts or beliefs as investigated by Philosophy, which we have not yet noticed: viz. that they are assumed to be true and valid. This is obviously involved in the view of Theoretical Philosophy as systematising the sciences; since a science is a system of true beliefs: so far as any actual science as taught is not this, it is imperfect or spurious science. So again Practical Philosophy is in

---

[1] The assertion 'All is Feeling' is a philosophical, not a psychological proposition, as the assertion 'All is Matter' is a philosophical and not a physical proposition.

intention a theory of the principles of what 'really' ought to be; *i.e.* not of what men merely think or judge ought to be, but of what they truly so think or judge. Philosophy therefore is concerned primarily with truth, and only secondarily with error in order to distinguish it from truth, or to elicit the element of truth contained in it. Psychology on the other hand has for its function to discriminate, analyse into elements, classify, and ascertain the laws of all such beliefs or thoughts as are found among the phenomena of the particular minds observed; of the false no less than the true. For instance, in studying laws of association of ideas, the associations that lead the mind to wrong judgment and expectation are just as interesting as those that lead to right judgment and expectation; and may even sometimes be more interesting and more instructive examples of the laws of association. Indeed the characteristic of being true or untrue is not one which necessarily claims our attention—so far at least as the true or untrue beliefs are not psychological beliefs—so long as we are merely concerned with mind as the object of a special science, abstracted as far as possible from the objects of other sciences.

But further: even so far as Philosophy and Psychology are both concerned with true beliefs, still from the point of view of either study respectively these beliefs are connected and systematised in ways *primâ facie* different. The general aim of Psychology, in the systematisation that it attempts of mental facts, is—besides classifying them,—to discover the laws of co-existence and sequence among them: accordingly, so far as it is concerned with knowledge or true beliefs, it aims at ascertaining the order in which and the processes by which the particular minds observed actually pass from one part of knowledge to another. On the other hand, the aim of Philosophy, in dealing with the same beliefs, is to arrange them in such order as may make manifest the important permanent relations among them,—*e.g.* the relations of the simple to the complex, of the more general to the less general, of the fundamental principles of any science to their applications or the deductions founded on them. Relations of this latter kind are, speaking broadly, the same for all minds that think and judge truly respecting them; whereas the former may and do vary from one mind to another, and include sequences of thought other than valid or cogent inference.

In connexion with this I may observe that in my view Philosophy—so far as it does not construct its system, or aim at constructing it completely *a priori* —uses primarily what I may call the Dialectical Method,[1] *i.e.* the method of reflection on the thought which we all share, by the aid of the symbolism which we all share, language: whereas Psychology uses primarily the introspective method of observation by each of his own thoughts and feelings as his own—a group of objects of which he alone can have first-hand knowledge. I do not mean that Philosophy may not

---

[1] Observe that the term is used in the Platonic-Aristotelian, and not in the Hegelian sense.

use the introspective method, or that Psychology may not use the dialectical, or that the two can be completely separated. But so far as the Philosopher observes the relations of thought in his own individual mind, it is as a means to the end of ascertaining the relations of thought in a normal mind, free from the peculiarities and limitations of his own individual mind. On the other hand, so far as the Psychologist adopts the method of reflecting on the common thought of the society to which he belongs, through the symbolism of its common language, it is as a means to the end of generalisations applicable to the particular experiences of an indefinite number of particular minds. Hence we may put the difference in another form, and say that Psychology is primarily concerned with knowledge and its attainment as processes of thought belonging to particular human minds; but that Philosophy is primarily concerned with the relations of true or valid beliefs as they may be conceived to exist for an ideal mind independent—not only of the errors but —of the particularities of growth and development of particular finite minds.[1]

It may, however, be suggested that—just as it is impossible properly to know the conclusion of a geometrical demonstration, without going through

---

[1] I do not mean that Philosophy ignores this growth and development: it is a fact of great importance about the Universe that the finite minds it includes go through processes of growth and development and attain truth by long series of steps. Still Philosophy, I conceive, is primarily concerned with the relations of the truths apprehended, as they exist in and for the most fully developed minds.

the steps of the demonstration—so, speaking more generally, it is impossible to know truth truly, unless we have arrived at it through a certain process; and that therefore the process by which the human mind has arrived at scientific or philosophical truth is an essential part—or at least introduction—to the truth known. But it is evident that in many cases of scientific truth this suggestion would be paradoxical; since an important part of the progress made in mathematics, *e.g.*, consists in the discovery of better ways of arriving at truths already known; and it would seem absurd to say that it is indispensable to a knowledge of the truth to know both these ways of arriving at it—the older and worse way as well as the newer and better way. If there is an ideal order of development of truth, it would seem therefore to be distinct from the actual order in which it has been historically developed in the progress of human civilisation. On the bearing of the investigation of the actual growth and development of human thought and belief—with which Psychology is concerned— on the investigation of its ideal order and connexion, which is the primary business of Philosophy, I shall have to speak more fully hereafter in the latter part of this course; as this is an investigation where Psychology at a certain point passes over into Sociology—or at any rate becomes Sociological Psychology.

§ 3. I now pass to compare the different ways in which the two studies are concerned with the relation of mind to the material world. It is evident that it will be an important part of the task of Philosophy

—according to the view I have taken of Philosophy—to conceive this relation with adequate precision and completeness. At the same time Psychology equally cannot ignore it: for though the method of Psychology is primarily introspective, it has in recent times become continually more clear that the study cannot dispense with the aid of physiological observation and reasoning.

The attempt that till recently was sometimes made by students of mind, to mark off a department of mental phenomena, elevated above the condition of being accompanied by nervous change, is now, I think, generally abandoned even by the psychologists who are most strongly opposed to materialism. It is generally admitted that we have overwhelming—though to a considerable extent highly inferential—grounds for believing that psychical facts such as sensations, emotions, thoughts, volitions, have always corporeal concomitants in movements of nerve-matter. And when this is admitted, the importance to the Psychologist of knowing all that can be known about these corporeal concomitants is hardly to be doubted.

On the other hand, the crude materialism or positivism that used to push aside all results of introspective observation has now mostly given way before the general recognition that psychical changes are, as objects of experience, altogether distinct from the nervous changes that accompany them. Since Descartes, philosophical thought has found no difficulty in distinguishing the thinking, feeling, willing thing, that each one of us is conscious of being, from the complex aggregate of extended solid particles which each of us calls his body. And if, neglecting the permanent, we fix our attention on the transient facts, the successive states or movements of mind and body, there is general agreement as to the profound disparity between thoughts or feelings and those nervous processes which appear to be inseparable from them, and which—in the case of Sensation—we sometimes call by the same name. As Spencer says, we are "utterly incapable of seeing or even imagining how the two are related . . . mind remains a something without any kinship with other things." On this ground I think Spencer's phrase, that " mind and nervous action are the subjective and objective *faces of the same thing,*" [1] is objectionable. For the image suggests that the manner of connexion between the two so-called 'faces' is manifest and their separation inconceivable: whereas according to Spencer's own statement the mode of connexion is occult and unimaginable, and the separation is so far from being inconceivable, that in the case of all the higher mental states we have no direct consciousness at all of the nervous change in the brain which we believe to take place as a concomitant of thought: we can only vaguely imagine it. Hence I am unable to take even this moderate step towards that extreme materialism which refuses to recognise the distinctness of physical and psychical fact. I have admitted

---

[1] Cf. *Principles of Psychology*, § 56. Cf. also Bain, *Mind and Body*, p. 134, "The mental fact is a two-sided fact."

that Materialism is in one sense philosophical : *i.e.* that it is the result of that effort after a complete systematising of knowledge which in the first lecture I called philosophy. But the *primâ facie* disparateness of mental facts and nervous changes, the apparently total absence of kinship between them, puts in the way of any materialistic systematisation an obstacle difficult to overleap.

Indeed I think that instructed thinkers of a materialistic tendency have now ceased to try to leap over this obstacle. At the present time the important issue between such thinkers and their opponents does not relate to the nature of the double facts with which psychology deals, or to the connexion of their disparate elements, psychical and physical— which no one professes to understand—but rather to the causal *nexus* that links each successive double fact with physical or psychical antecedents or consequents. What the materialistic thinker maintains and his opponent denies is that this causal *nexus* is to be conceived as lying wholly on the physical side; and that psychical facts are merely unexplained effects or epiphenomena, and not in their turn even part-causes of physical facts; in other words, that studying the succession of psycho-physical facts—thoughts and feelings accompanied by movements in the nerve-matter of the brain—we ought to conceive the causal *nexus* of the facts as lying wholly on the physical side, and ultimately to be explained by purely physical laws.

This is a problem which is—I think we may say—

in the forefront of speculative interest at the present time, for educated persons generally, and not merely for special students of Philosophy or of Psychology: and it seems to me of great importance to distinguish the questions capable of being solved by the methods of the empirical sciences Psychology and Physiology combined, from those which carry us beyond the limits of these sciences, and therefore must be reserved for Philosophy. Now it does not fall within my plan here to inquire whether the proposition that physical changes must be wholly caused by antecedent physical changes is true or false; my point is that the question is one which cannot be solved either by Physiology or Psychology or both together regarded as purely empirical studies; and should therefore be left to Philosophy. For the question whether the psychical facts — thoughts, feelings and volitions — which in the case of ordinary conscious actions are certainly among the *antecedents* of physical change, have strictly speaking any causal connexion with these changes—this question cannot be determined by any physiological observation and experiment. We have to consider on the one hand the presumption arising from the continuity of the organic with the inorganic world, and of human life with other organic life so far as the operation of mechanical laws is the same in all three departments. However much stress is laid on the difference between the organic and the inorganic world, and between human and non-human life, no one seriously doubts the complete subjection of the whole physical world to the law of gravitation and the law of conservation of energy. We have to consider on the other hand the validity of the consciousness of activity—implied in the universally accepted distinction between 'active' and 'passive' in our mental states, and especially of the consciousness of *'free'* activity, which seems irrestibility forced on us by reflection on deliberate action. Then as regards this latter, we have to take Ethics into account, and the connexion of Duty and Freedom.

Hence, as I said, the problem of the exact causal *nexus* between the successive psycho-physical facts, with their twofold character, is one for Philosophy. It can hardly be said to be not a psychological question: I conceive, however, that the empirical psychologist may properly leave this controversy on one side, and that on the whole it is better that he should leave it to Philosophy: the empirical psychologist may content himself with tracing uniformities of co-existence and sequence among the psychical facts that he studies, taken along with their physical accompaniments and antecedents, without entering further into the question of their causation.

It is convenient here to distinguish two points of view from which the relations between physical and psychical facts are to be studied, in the empirical sciences of Psychology and Sociology. We may term these respectively the Psycho-Physiological and the Biological. There is not a sharp line to be drawn between the two, but the general distinction is clear. From the former point of view we examine, as closely as possible, the particular physical changes—primarily the movements of particles of the nervous system —which accompany, or closely precede or follow particular kinds of psychical facts, sensations, thoughts, emotions; also taking note of movements of matter outside the organism which immediately affect the nervous system, and constitute the stimuli of the organs of sense. From the Biological point of view, on the other hand, we consider the general effects of the physical conditions under which the organism lives on the development of mental faculties: *e.g.* we observe how the need of obtaining food and avoiding or resisting foes has developed and differentiated faculties of perception along with organs of sense, and faculties and habits of complex purposive action along with similarly complex organs for exercising force on the external world. It is with this latter kind of consideration that the sociologist is chiefly concerned: for instance, he observes how the advantages of gregariousness in the physical struggle for existence develop habits of co-operation, and communication by vocal signs or otherwise,—and ultimately the sympathy and mutual intelligence which render the mental life of man essentially a social life. For the present I shall confine myself to the Psycho-Physiological point of view.

It is hardly necessary to show in detail, how Physiological knowledge—and even, to some extent, physical knowledge going beyond Physiology — is indispensable in examining the causes of psychical facts introspectively observed. We have to examine the relation between different kinds of sensation, and processes of nervous action stimulated by the motions of inorganic matter coming into contact with the organs of sense—vibrations of the luminiferous ether with the retina of the eye, vibrations of the air with the ear, etc. We have to examine how the quantity, quality, and duration of the feeling are related first to the process of change in the nerves, and to the nature and organisation of the nervous matter to which the external stimuli are applied, and secondly to the kind, amount, and order of these stimuli. Then —when we go on to consider the laws according to which a combination of these sensations, and of secondary states which appear faintly to reproduce them, bring into being mental phenomena of a more complicated kind,—though Physiology can give us less direct aid, still it is well always to bear in mind that our psychological questions and hypotheses have physiological counterparts. Association of ideas, fusion of sensations and their images or relics into more complex states, memory, recollection, imagination, even reasoning and judgment, must be assumed to have physiological bases; the existence of which we must always keep in view, though we must bear in mind also that their specific character is unknown, and only to be vaguely conjectured. Further, Physiology will aid Psychology, not merely in the way of supplementing the results of introspective observation with a knowledge of the physical antecedents, concomitants and effects of psychological phenomena; but also more directly by showing where to look for psychical facts—such as muscular feelings—which come into view when attention is adequately concentrated on them, but are liable to remain undistinguished in ordinary introspective observation. In view of the importance of this aid, it is difficult to limit the extent to which psychological analysis may be advanced by the progress of physiological knowledge.

In discussing the relation of Psychology to Physiology, I have incidentally illustrated the kind of questions which, in my view, belong to Philosophy as the study that aims at systematising the methods and conclusions of the special sciences. So far as *this* relation of Mind to Matter is concerned, the work of Philosophy in co-ordinating the sciences consists largely in preventing either *confusion* or *collision* between diverse methods, and in delineating the path of harmonious co-operation. But I have had another aim in dwelling upon this relation: I wish to bring out clearly the distinction between this and another quite different relation of Mind to Matter, which we have next to consider.

Not only is some material process—as we have overwhelming ground for believing—an invariable accompaniment of every mental process: but at the same time the mental process may be a cognition that has matter for its object. And it is important to see clearly that the movement of nerve-particles in the brain, which accompanies the transient psychical fact that we call cognition, is usually altogether different from the matter that we are thinking about. Thus:

I see that table. Here is a psychical fact—perception of table—which we believe to be related to matter in two ways; (1) to some unknown change in the matter of my brain as its immediate antecedent and concomitant, and (2) to the table as object; these are obviously two very different material facts.

I lay stress on this difference, because in psychological and philosophical discussions of Perception, there is some tendency to confound the two relations of mind to matter; and so, by mixing up the material concomitant or antecedent of cognition with its object, to fail of obtaining a clear notion of either. Thus it is sometimes said that what I 'really see' is the image on the retina, or perhaps the undulations of the luminiferous ether in contact with the eye. But reflection will show that neither of these facts is *either* the immediate antecedent or concomitant of vision *or* its immediate object. It is not its immediate antecedent or concomitant, because the nerve-process has many stages to pass through from the retina inwards before vision takes place: while, again, it is not its immediate object, because in vision I do not directly learn anything about the image on the retina of the thing seen or about the ethereal undulations: I only know these physical facts as the result, in the one case of a quite different observation, in the other case of a long process of scientific reasoning.

§ 4. We have now to observe that out of the double relation of Mind to Matter, which I have been explaining, arise the contrasted systems of (1) Materialism and (2) what is often called Idealism—

but I think it better to call it Mentalism, reserving the term Idealism, in accordance with recent usage, for a particular species of Mentalism. Materialism takes exclusive hold of one end by which mind is tied to matter, and identifies the thought or feeling with the nerve-process that accompanies it : Mentalism takes exclusive hold of the other end, and analyses matter as an object of perception and thought into mental elements. But the Materialistic resolution of mind into matter is only acceptable when we think loosely and confusedly : to the steady gaze of reflection the psychical phenomenon which it is sought to absorb into the physical always returns distinct and quite disparate from it. The Mentalistic explanation of matter in terms of mind has a much more profound and subtle plausibility. No one practised in reflective analysis can admit that what he means by a thought is a change in the grey or other matter of his brain : but it is more difficult to show that what I mean by (say) a table is anything else than an aggregate of feelings, actual or possible (*i.e.* ideal), and of thoughts binding the feelings together.

This analysis I now propose to examine : but before examining it, we should note that it is pursued by three different classes of thinkers to three very different kinds of result. I will briefly characterise these three classes, taking the simplest types, and overlooking intermediate shades and combinations.

The first class are not strictly to be termed

Mentalists, but rather perhaps Phenomenalists or Relativists: for though they analyse matter, as an object of perception and knowledge, into mental elements, they do not conclude that matter does not exist independently of mind, but only that we can have no knowledge of it as so existing; we can only, they hold, know how it appears to mind. The pure Mentalists go a step further and deny the existence of this unknown and unknowable matter: the ultimate reality—as they agree in holding—is mental or psychical in its nature. But while one section of them regard reality as ultimately Feeling—reducing somehow the *relational* element in our common notion of the physical world to a secondary and derivative kind of feeling—another section holds that, so far as the Real is definitely knowable, its main or sole constituent is Thought. The former it seems best to call Sensationalists (bearing in mind that this term is sometimes used for a confused blending of sensationalistic mentalism with Materialism): for the latter—of whom Green is an example—I reserve the term Idealist.

This classification, as you will see, belongs to Philosophy rather than to Psychology. It is the business of Psychology to consider how far the transient mental fact which we call a cognition or thought of a portion of matter is capable of being analysed into elements and what these elements are: and this no doubt has a *bearing* on the question 'whether matter, as we commonly conceive it, exists independently of mind.' But it belongs to Philosophy, not to Psychology, to *decide* this latter question.[1]

In examining the analysis of our cognition or notion of matter—*i.e.* of matter as commonly conceived, 'phenomenal' matter—it is important to distinguish three different methods; (*a*) Empirical Reflective Analysis, (*b*) Psychogonical Analysis, and (*c*) Transcendental Analysis, which carries us beyond the limits of empirical Psychology. The first is used more or less by all thinkers; the use of the second is characteristic of Relativists and Sensationalists; the use of the third is peculiar to Idealists. In the present lecture I wish to concentrate attention on the results of the first two methods.

(*a*) Firstly, direct reflection shows us that certain percepts which in ordinary thought we regard as located in the material world, outside our bodies, are in part not definitely attached to this material world, and are at any rate not essential to our notion of matter. Thus sounds, smells, flavours are not definitely attached to any portion of matter outside

[1] It may be thought that in this and the following section I am arguing definitely the metaphysical question at issue between Mentalism and Common Sense; so that when the end of these sections is reached I conceive the question to be settled. But this would be altogether premature. The issues between Common Sense and Mentalism in different forms are among the most important and extensively discussed in modern metaphysical controversy— indeed they are only surpassed in importance by the questions that lead into Theology—and we are only now in the vestibule of metaphysics and making our way towards it. What I am here arriving at is something quite different: I am considering how far empirical Psychology, as a special science, will take us in the discussion of this controversy; and I am considering this because it seems to me that Mentalists—especially 'Psychological Philosophers'—have fallen into the mistake of supposing that it will take us further than it will.

the organism; and we can perfectly well conceive matter as flavourless, inodorous, non-resonant. In fact careful reflection leads me to distinguish—as regards (*e.g.*) Sound—between a sensation of sound, which so far as it is connected with any matter is connected with the nervous system of my ear and brain, and a process of material particles outside: and when this distinction is made clear, I no longer attribute Sound—as distinct from motion of material particles—to the matter outside.

The case of colour is different, as this percept is definitely extended and attached to the surface of matter: I cannot conceive colour unextended. But colour depends on light; and so much of my life is spent in the dark, that I can easily conceive a world without light or colour, in which my perception of matter would depend entirely on touch and the muscular sense: and I am helped in this conception by the physical theory of light, since the movements of the luminiferous ether which affect my optical nerves are inevitably conceived to be movements of lightless and colourless matter.

In this way reflective analysis enables me to separate from my notion of matter as it exists independently of mind what used to be called the *Secondary Qualities* of matter: *i.e.* the percepts of the special senses, taste, smell, hearing, and sight.

Then, after having gone so far, it is easy, in reflecting on such qualities as hard, soft, smooth, rough, etc., to distinguish elements which belong to the sense of touch and the muscular sense, and which we can separate from our notion of matter as it exists outside our organism and not affecting it. Let us take the notions of 'hard,' 'soft,' 'rough,' 'smooth,' and reflect on their meaning. There is no doubt, I suppose, that we commonly regard them as attributes of various portions of matter existing in space outside our organisms: at the same time there seems no doubt that each term suggests a faint image of a particular quality of complex sensation—of touch, pressure and muscular sense combined—which I experience when one of my bodily organs, *e.g.* a finger, presses against a portion of matter called hard or soft, or is moved along the surface of a portion called rough or smooth. Now it seems to me that psychological reflection enables us to distinguish the quality of hardness, etc.—conceived as existing in the thing apart from any contact with our own or any other sentient organism—from the sensations of which I have spoken. I can make the distinction, because if I conceive a hard piece of inorganic matter (A) colliding with another hard piece (B) and then afterwards with a soft piece (C), the difference of its effect on each I conceive to manifest the hardness of (B) and the softness of (C); although there is no effect conceived to be produced on any sentient organism. I thus see that by 'hardness' as a quality of matter existing independently of organic feeling, I mean a tendency to preserve its form and internal structure—spatial relations—comparatively unchanged when it comes into collision with matter; and by 'softness' a tendency to change them with comparative ease under similar circumstances.

In this way I separate the elements of imaginary tactual sensation from my notion of matter conceived as 'hard,' etc., and thus distinguish in thought my notion of extended matter from my notion of tactual sensation, and conceive the former as existing apart from the latter.

At this point it may be answered, "No doubt one can think of bodies other than his own organism and of transactions between such bodies as having an objective existence, but then I inevitably think of such bodies as tangible and resisting: the content of my conception of matter cannot be separated from actual or imaginary sensations belonging to the sense of touch and the muscular sense." Now I am willing to agree with this statement up to a certain point—or rather to agree with a statement which will approach somewhat near to this. I find that when I fix my thought upon 'extended matter,' and endeavour to contemplate reflectively and definitely the fact signified by this name, imaginary sensations of my own, visual, tactual, muscular, etc., come into my thought—visual I think at least as much as tactual, but certainly both: and I have no objection to grant that I cannot while dwelling on the notion of 'extension' or 'extended matter' effectually exclude such imaginary sensations from my consciousness. So much I concede to the objector. But granting that I cannot exclude them from my contemplative consciousness, it seems to me no less certain that I can and always do exclude them from my conception of material reality, as existing independently of my consciousness.

Just as, in reading a vivid narrative of an ancient event of historic interest—say a battle in the Peloponnesian war or a debate in the Roman Senate—I am apt to imagine myself present, and seeing and hearing what goes on: nay, if the story is vividly told, I may be even carried further in imagination and partially imagine myself one of the actors in the scene. But all this play of imagination goes on without in the least altering my conception of the historic fact: I know all the while that the men whose actions and sufferings thus excite my imaginative sympathy lived ages ago when I (so far as I know) was non-existent. Similarly when I try to conceive vividly the planetary system—as modern astronomers lead me to conceive it—emerging from the primitive nebula, I have imaginary visual sensations, and when I try to imagine its rotation, imaginary muscular sensations, but I do not for a moment suppose that there were any such sensations, at a time when, as I suppose, there were not any sentient organisms. So again, when I think (*e.g.*) of the attraction of gravitation operating within our Solar System: of the sun drawing the earth and being drawn by it, the earth drawing the moon and being drawn by it, I find I usually have a faint imagination of muscular effort connected with the notion of drawing or pulling: but I do not really attribute this feeling—in the very least degree—to the sun, or the moon, or the earth.

Well, this is my answer to this line of objection. I grant a certain normal connexion between my conception no less than my perception of extended matter and real or imaginary sensations, visual, tactual, or muscular: but it is not a connexion which in any way impedes my conceiving of extended matter as it exists apart from sensation.

Accordingly I analyse the common notions of 'hard,' 'soft,' 'smooth,' 'rough,' etc., into:—(1) a sensational complex, actual or imaginary, composed of elements belonging to muscular sense as well as to the sense of touch; (2) a cognition, presentative or representative, of relational qualities of matter as it exists independently of my perception. I say 'relational qualities,' because the meaning of the term 'hard' *e.g.* involves a relation between the portion of matter cognised as hard and some other matter supposed to come into collision with it: but this other matter need not be a part of my or any other organism.

I admit that when I first fix my attention on the thought of extended matter, endeavouring to realise what I mean by the term, and then reflect on my state of consciousness when this endeavour is made, I find that my imaginary sensations, visual, tactual, muscular, are normally elements of my state of consciousness, and cannot be excluded. But my contention is that I do not in my ordinary thought attribute to them any representative validity: they come in as elements of my conscious state, not as elements of my conception of material reality as existing independently of my consciousness.

Here, however, direct reflective analysis stops. There remains in our notion of matter—stripped as bare of sensational elements as direct reflective analysis can strip it—the properties which Hamilton distinguishes as 'Geometrical Solidity,' and 'Physical Solidity' or Incompressibility. I cannot separate from my notion of matter the 'necessity of trinal extension, in length, breadth, and thickness,' and I cannot conceive that the matter thus extended can be reduced to the condition of being non-extended; I must conceive it as ultimately incompressible.

(b) What I have called *Psychogonical Analysis* now takes up the work. It starts with the result which direct analysis yields—that the percepts of the different senses, though actually attached to our notion of matter in ordinary thought, are found to be separable from it by direct reflection, aided by physical theory: and it raises the question, How did this combination of percepts and concepts, which we can reflectively unravel, come about?

The answer is, By a process of association of percepts and images, carried on before the stage of conscious reflection and leading to the formation, after repeated occurrences of associated sense-perceptions, of the complex state of consciousness which constitutes our present conception of things as coloured, resonant, and odorous. Then further, the doctrine of evolution and heredity enables us to carry back this process beyond the range of the individual's life. But thus carrying it back, we may be induced to carry it further than reflective analysis carries the process of separation. We may be induced to suppose that even our percepts and concepts of Extension and Solidity are similarly formed by associations of sensations of touch—with sensations of sight co-operating—and sensations of the muscular sense. In this way our whole thought of the material world may be hypothetically traced back to sensational elements.

§ 5. Now if I were giving a course of lectures on Psychology regarded as a special science, I should have some critical remarks to make on the assumptions underlying this conjectural history; in particular, it seems to me a fundamental error, in thinking of earlier mental states, to carry back hypothetically into them the clear distinctions of later thought, as the Psychogonist is liable to do. But this is not now our business: I am not concerned therefore to criticise the process of psychogonical reasoning which I have summarily given, so far as it is put forward merely as a description of the manner in which the faculty of perceiving and conceiving material things as we now do has gradually been developed, as an account *i.e.* of the sensational *antecedents* of which these perceptions and conceptions are consequents.

But this is not the conclusion that the Relativist or Sensationalist draws from this reasoning. The conclusion he draws is that these feelings are not merely antecedents of our common notion of the material world, but elements of which it is composed:

that therefore through our common notion of the material world we do not know anything at all of that world as it really is independent of our minds: we only know a complex mental fact.

Now I think that this conclusion, in the first place, is quite unwarranted by the reasoning on which it is based, and secondly, that it is palpably inconsistent with the assumptions made in that reasoning itself. The first of these points I have already argued in the parallel case of ethics: I have tried to show that in the application of psychogonical analysis to resolve moral cognition and disinterested choice into more primitive mental facts, there is a fundamental confusion between antecedents and elements.[1] If, however, this process is unwarrantable and fallacious in dealing with ethical notions, it is doubly unwarrantable in the case of physical notions. For here inconsistency is added to fallacy. The moralist who explains away altruism into egoism, or rational choice into instinctive impulse, is not obliged,—in order to carry through the process of psychogonical explanation—to assume as actually existing at earlier stages the altruism or the rational choice to which he is leading up as the result of the development. But this is what the Relativist or Sensationalist has to do in the process by which he explains away matter into feeling. For in tracing the manner in which sensations belonging to different senses—primarily feelings of touch and feelings that attend the exercise of muscles, secondarily visual feelings — combine

[1] *Methods of Ethics*, 6th ed., p. 32: see also pp. 211-213.

to form the notion of solid matter in space of three dimensions, he does not confine himself to Psychology proper, and think only of sensation and sense regarded as psychical facts. On the contrary he brings into marked prominence the physical side of sense and sensations; indeed, he talks so much of the organs of sense, the brain, and the nerve-processes, that his explanation to ordinary readers presents itself as a *materialistic* explanation. This is the case (*e.g.*) with Spencer: he justly repudiates the idea that he is a materialist; but I always feel that the simple reader may be excused for the mistake; owing to the prominence that Spencer gives to the physiological side of the processes of development that he traces. Throughout his exposition, from first to last, the reader's thought, being kept fixed on the organic processes preceding and accompanying mental feelings, is kept within the world of matter in space, the particles of which are conceived by him to be existing, moving and operating apart from any cognition by mind of their existence and operation:—for the developing mind contemplated is certainly not conscious of the processes going on in its brain and nervous system. How is it possible, then, that the result of this process can be to deprive of their objective validity these fundamental conceptions of space, motion, and mass which have been used throughout the process? The inconsistency seems to me flagrant and palpable.

But why, it may be asked, does not the Relativist or Sensationalist see this?

I think that his failure to see it is partly due to the want of clear and steady perception of the duality of the relation between mind and matter which I explained earlier in this lecture. Not having this duality clearly before his mind, the Relativist in thinking of matter in one relation, forgets that matter at the same time is coming into his thought on the other side: his attention and analysis are primarily occupied with the relation of mind to matter as object perceived; and the relation of mental changes to nervous changes which accompany them but are not their object—this steals into and even becomes prominent in his thought without his noticing that in contemplating this relation and tracing it through the complications which his theory involves, he is assuming real matter in real space as naïvely as the plain man assumes it in the case of more ordinary perceptions.

And one reason why I before laid so much stress on the indispensability, increasingly felt in Psychological study, of obtaining the aid of Physiology, is because this shows that the tendency of psychological study is in the direction of making the inconsistency of which I speak continually more prominent. The unphysiological psychologist, who lets his brain, nerves, and sense-organs drop into the background of his thought, may more easily explain away into mental elements the matter which he conceives only as *object* of perception. But he now represents a past stage of psychological theory: and the psycho-physiologist, or physiological psychologist who represents the present tendency of psychological investigation must find this explanation continually more difficult.

Perhaps it may be replied, "No doubt the physiological psychologist must assume the real existence of *some* kind of matter: but not of the matter ordinarily conceived and apparently perceived by the plain man. The matter which the man of science assumes is no doubt conceived to occupy space in some manner, and to change its position in space, but the duly instructed man of science recognises— what the plain man does not see, or only dimly sees —that the ultimate constitution of matter is a problem not yet solved. Whether matter consists ultimately of absolutely solid particles, or of centres of force— or possibly, as Lord Kelvin suggested, vortices in a primitive fluid, having no other properties than inertia, invariable density, and perfect mobility—these questions the judicious physicist does not pretend to answer definitely or decisively; he would even admit that every particular answer that can be given is exposed to grave difficulties. Even the law of gravitation itself, when we reflect on it, strikingly exemplifies the imperfection of our present conceptions of the world without us. *Prima facie*, it involves the notion of attractive force exercised at a distance, and not propagated through motion of particles of an intervening medium: but it has so far been found impossible to bring this into harmony with the rest of our systematised experience of the manner in which forces operate on masses. With so great and palpable incoherence in our system of physical conceptions, is it not absurd to maintain that we know matter as it really is?"

No doubt all this, and more, might be said by a sceptical physicist against the *finality* of the present conceptions which science presents to us of the material world. But this is no argument for Mentalism as against Natural Dualism; unless the mentalist is prepared to contend that our conception of mind is free from similar incoherences—which few mentalists are at present hardy enough to maintain. Nor does it prove the 'Relativity of knowledge,' in any useful sense of the word 'Relativity': it only proves its imperfection. And the Natural Dualist may fairly urge that the imperfection of our physical knowledge has been continually reduced in the progress of physical science: and that this improvement has been effected, not by throwing aside the plain man's conception of matter as a reality independent of mind, but by working on it, purging it from elements that reflection shows to be clearly subjective, and bringing it, together with the connected notions of space, force, and motion, into continually clearer consistency and closer harmony with experience. This defence of Common Sense is, I think, valid against any conclusions drawn from Psychogonical analysis; but we have yet to consider whether this or any other defence will avail against Transcendental analysis. This consideration, however, I must reserve for a subsequent lecture.[1]

[1] Cf. below, pp. 81*f*, 91*f*.

LECTURE IV

THE SCOPE OF METAPHYSICS

§ 1. In the preceding lectures we have considered the Scope of Philosophy in relation successively to:

(1) Sciences or 'Positive Sciences.'

(2) Arts and Practical Studies — Ethics and Politics.

(3) Psychology.

In the course of this inquiry we have been led, by the mere effort to give a comprehensive definition of the Scope of Philosophy, to note various *primâ facie* one-sided views.

(*a*) Materialistic Philosophy, which does not recognise Mind—at any rate as an object of scientific knowledge—except as a complex mode of matter in motion.

(*b*) Naturalistic or Positive Philosophy, which does not recognise what ought to be as an object of knowledge, distinct from the knowledge of the existences and sequences of phenomena.

(*c*) Psychological Philosophy, which regards the knowable world as consisting, when analysed into ultimate elements, of mental fact: and—in the case of the division of this school which has especially applied to its method the term 'psychological'—regards the ultimate elements as being the '*feelings*' actual and possible of particular minds—using the word *feeling* in a wide sense to include sensation as well as emotion.

I call these views *primâ facie* one-sided, because they neglect or obliterate important distinctions which we find in our common thought, and which I conceive we ought to take note of in defining the subjects—however much we may be ultimately disposed to treat them as subordinate.

In the first part of this survey—in considering the relation of Philosophy to Sciences and Arts, we came near Metaphysics without taking note of it: it was there, but it did not come distinctly into view. But in trying to make clear and precise the distinction between Philosophy and Psychology we found ourselves drawn into this central region of Philosophical study. For though it is possible to keep clear of metaphysics in our empirical investigation of the relation of states of consciousness to their physiological antecedents and concomitants, it is not possible to keep clear of it in considering the relation of Mind to Matter as our object of thought: the distinctions I tried to indicate, between various 'isms'—Natural Dualism, Mentalism, Idealism, Sensationalism—were, as my audience doubtless perceived, Metaphysical distinctions. The time has therefore clearly come to concentrate attention more directly on the effort to define the scope of Metaphysics.

The definition of the scope of Metaphysics presents peculiar difficulties: partly owing to a widespread doubt whether such a study ought to exist. We are all agreed that there are such bodies of systematic knowledge as the Sciences:—we may dispute how far they are valuable or complete, but that their methods are in the main valid, and their results real knowledge, no competent judge seriously doubts. The case is otherwise, as we saw, with Philosophy: but when Philosophy is explained to be aiming at co-ordination and systematisation of the Sciences, it is generally admitted that its work is possible and desirable, though it may be at present in a rudimentary state, —at any rate we are not thought to be transgressing the limits of the human intellect in trying to achieve it. But there is a widespread idea that Metaphysicians are guilty of such transgression: consequently the term is not unfrequently used in a bad sense, to denote inquiries which experience has shown to be futile. This is not my view: I think that the questions, which—according to the traditional meaning of the word—it is convenient to distinguish as metaphysical, are, in part at least, questions to which as rational beings we are bound to seek some kind of answer;—though we may have to content ourselves with a very imperfect and provisional answer. And whether we pursue Metaphysics or not, I think it important to ascertain clearly the place that the knowledge it seeks would occupy in a complete scheme of human knowledge.

The disparaging use of the term, then, must be

faced and allowed for: accordingly I try to find a definition which will suit both friends and foes of Metaphysics. That is, I do not omit questions that the human mind seems to me strongly impelled to ask, merely because thinkers of influence have pronounced them futile. Here, however, you may think that the method I proposed, in the case of Philosophy, to find a definition acceptable to all schools—by concentrating attention on the *questions* Philosophy asks instead of the answers given by philosophers—can hardly be applied; because I admit that important thinkers hold that the questions Metaphysics asks ought not to be asked. But the interest of the questions is, as I have said, too profound to allow them to be simply ignored: so that even those philosophers who refuse to ask the questions have to give a reason for their refusal.

Thus if they do not admit the questions directly within the scope of their study, they have to admit them indirectly by investigating the previous question whether they ought to be investigated. For example, Spencer holds as a fundamental doctrine that 'the power which the Universe manifests to us is utterly inscrutable,' and devotes several chapters to establishing it. The discussion of these chapters I call metaphysical.

Let us then, in order to define the *boundaries* of this study, briefly survey its *confines;*—the other studies with which it is liable to be partially confounded, but from which, in common usage, it is more or less vaguely distinguished.[1] (1) The distinction between Metaphysics and Physics has to be made clear—since it is evident that Metaphysics aims at knowledge of some kind about the material world. The vulgar are aware that the Metaphysician asks 'what is matter' as well as 'what is mind.' (2) On the other hand, Metaphysics has to to be distinguished in some way from Philosophy. This distinction is obscurer in ordinary thought; probably many of the persons who distinguish Philosophy from Science would identify it with Metaphysics. I think, however, that there is a preponderance of usage in favour of including Metaphysics within Philosophy, as a part or kind of philosophy; as it is generally understood that there is a manner of philosophising which claims to be 'Positive,' in contrast to 'Metaphysical.'[2] So,

---

[1] Here, as in many similar cases, inquiries into original derivation will not much help us. For there is no doubt that the use of the term 'Metaphysics' is derived from the title of a treatise of Aristotle's, that was not given to this treatise by Aristotle himself. Aristotle himself calls the subject 'First Philosophy' or 'Theology' or 'Philosophy about divine things': the Greek title modernised into 'Metaphysics' was given to the treatise by a Peripatetic of the first century A.D., Andronicus Rhodius, who collected and arranged Aristotle's works; and perhaps it merely meant that the treatise came 'after Physics' in his arrangement.

In any case it would probably be better to start not from *original* but from *present* usage: for we may expect that the progress of knowledge, during the interval that separates us from Aristotle, will have caused existing thought to contain, at least implicitly, more and clearer distinctions than the thought of Aristotle.

[2] Fortunately the works of Comte and Spencer give us voluminous concrete examples of the difference. I will take Spencer as more familiar to our own time: I cannot say that Spencer, like Comte, really treats Metaphysics simply as a form of error: in fact he is not more interested in the Agnosticism of his 'First Principles' than he is in the 'Transfigured Realism' of his Principles of Psychology; and the latter is strictly meta-

again (3), the difference between Metaphysics and Psychology is now pretty widely recognised. We must allow, I think, a certain amount of common ground to the two subjects; but, if Metaphysics is taken to be a part or kind of Philosophy, the distinctions which in a previous lecture I drew between Philosophy and Psychology will apply here. Indeed the development of the older English Empirical Psychology, and especially the more recent development of experimental Psychology and Psychophysiology, have made current and familiar the conception of a kind of Psychology which is not metaphysical; on the other hand the spread of Kantian or Neo-Kantian doctrine in England has diffused intelligence of a kind of Metaphysics which claims but a slender connexion with Empirical Psychology.

To make the last point clearer, I may recall the distinction of methods which I gave in discussing the relation of Philosophy to Psychology. It would be generally agreed that (*a*) the method of direct reflective analysis—whether pursued with or without the aid of Physiology,—and (*b*) the psychogonical method,—whether pursued with or without the aid of comparative Zoology or Sociology,—are not, in the main, metaphysical. On the other hand the Transcendental Method—which endeavours to penetrate beyond the results of empirical reflection, by ascertaining the necessary conditions, not the

physical doctrine, though I find it difficult to make it agree with the former. But of the ten volumes of his Synthetic Philosophy, the whole of the *primâ facie* metaphysical discussion, if put together, would not occupy more than one: and the most interesting part of Spencer's work lies in the other nine.

historical antecedents, of our empirical knowledge— undoubtedly belongs to Metaphysics.

(4) Finally, a line has to be drawn between Metaphysics and Logic. Readers of Mill's *Logic* will be aware that the latter subject continually takes them up to the border of the former; indeed, they must be aware, too, that Mill sometimes takes them over this border, and therefore that the line is rather difficult to draw. But provisionally we may say that, while Logic is primarily concerned with the validity of Inference, the discussion of the validity of cognitions attained otherwise than by inference takes us into Metaphysics.

Let us, then, consider further these distinctions in order to get them as clear and precise as possible.

§ 2. To begin with the first and most obvious,— how shall we draw the line between Metaphysics and Physics? Firstly, since we have taken Metaphysics to be a part or kind of Philosophy, it is clear that it will not be concerned with detailed knowledge of the material world, but only with general propositions of fundamental importance relating to it. Still, this consideration will not furnish us with the distinction which we require; since there can hardly be a proposition more general or more important than the law of gravitation, which no one certainly would call metaphysical. Nor, again, is it sufficient to say that while Physics deals with matter so far as it is an object of external perception, Metaphysics considers it as an object of abstract thought; since theoretical mechanics does not exactly treat of matter as it is perceived, but of such matter ideally simplified for the convenience of abstract reasoning—perfectly smooth planes, perfectly rigid rods, etc. Probably the most generally accepted formula of distinction is that the propositions of Physics are always such as are somehow capable of 'empirical verification' or 'reduction to sensible experience,'—that is, such as admit or might admit of being proved or disproved, directly or indirectly, by some particular sense-perceptions, some apparently immediate knowledge of the external world, obtained by exercising one or more of the organs of sense; while propositions about matter that do not admit of this are metaphysical. And doubtless most of the questions that are now continually raised and settled in the progress of physical science are decided by observations of sensible facts:—by watching, measuring, weighing, testing in some way in which organs of sense are exercised. I propose, therefore, provisionally to accept this distinction, subject to additions or qualifications hereafter.[1]

The line thus drawn seems to correspond broadly to the current usage of the term 'Metaphysics.' The widest physical generalisations that keep within the range of physical science—such as the law of gravitation—are commonly conceived to rest upon an empirical basis: to be verified directly or indirectly by numberless observations and experiments that continually confirm their truth. This may be said even with regard to the belief in the conservation of

[1] Cf. below, p. 99.

mass and the conservation of energy. It was indeed held by Descartes and his followers that we could know *à priori*, by abstract reflection on the conception of matter as a substance, that the *quantum* of matter in the world always remains unchanged. But at any rate the proposition is indirectly verified by its correspondence with experience as collected and generalised by science; and it is on this verification that physicists would now commonly rely.

On the other hand there is a group of questions —highly interesting if they could be answered— which relate to the physical world, but clearly do not admit of a similar appeal to experience: such as whether the world is infinitely extended in space, or whether it had a beginning in time. These would be universally relegated to Metaphysics: and it seems clear that any one who is bold enough to answer these questions at all must do so on other than empirical grounds. The case is not so clear with regard to inquiries into the ultimate constitution of matter: the question whether its ultimate elements are to be conceived as incompressible bits of matter or in some other way may possibly some day meet with a solution based indirectly on experiment and observation. But this strengthens rather than weakens the distinction now drawn: since it would seem to be only in view of this possibility that the question of the ultimate constitution of matter is admitted by physicists as a legitimate subject even of speculation.

I do not mean that the general distinction is always easy to apply, or that we ought to regard its application as something fixed and final. On the contrary I think we may expect that, in the progress both of Physical Science and Psychology, questions that now seem beyond the range of empirical Science and are therefore left to Metaphysics may be brought within that range, probably after undergoing some transformation. Something of this kind seems to me to have happened with regard to this very question of the ultimate constitution of matter. A century ago this question—in the form 'whether matter is infinitely divisible or not'—seemed as much beyond the range of the methods of physical Science, as the questions already mentioned, which Kant classed along with it:—'whether the world had or had not a beginning in time' and 'whether it is or is not infinitely extended in space.' But though I assume that these latter would still, by the unanimous consent of men of science, be left to the Metaphysician, if he likes to discuss them, this is not the case with the question as to the ultimate constitution of matter: for this, no doubt in a changed form, has been the subject of keen and active discussion by physicists, which is—I understand—still going on. I assume that everybody has heard of the theory to which I chiefly refer—the theory that the ultimate element of matter is a vortex returning into itself and forming a closed ring in a homogeneous incompressible fluid identified with the ether of which the vibrations are supposed to constitute light. I understand that the conception of this vortex-ring will serve for the atom, in the sense in which Physics is interested in atoms:—*i.e.* for the physically indestructible element in all variations of physical change.

§ 3. Turning from Matter to Mind, we may similarly distinguish Metaphysics, so far as it is concerned with Mind, from Psychology regarded as an empirical study of Mind, proceeding by methods of observation, experiment, induction, analogous to those used in Physics. It is true that the difference here is subtler: since psychological reflection or introspection is less easily distinguished than sense-perception is from metaphysical reflection. But at any rate we may say that empirical Psychology is mainly concerned with the variable and particular elements of consciousness: whereas Metaphysics aims at determining the necessary or universal characteristics or conditions of Mind and Cognition. The question whether, as some thinkers have held, we can cognise empirically a universal and permanent self or ego—'presented as substance'—may be regarded as on the border-ground between Metaphysics and empirical Psychology. Here there is some controversy as to the content of psychical experience which the empirical psychologist analyses and classifies. I myself side with those who regard the self as object of immediate intuition. It seems to me that, introspectively, at any moment, with a certain exercise of memory, I perceive that I exist and perdure through changing states of consciousness. I know that I am, though I do not know what I am. But for the old view of certain dogmatic Metaphysicians that I perceive myself to be a self-subsistent entity and therefore indestructible by the forces that ultimately destroy my material organism —for this I find no warrant in introspection. This is how I divide the question of the substantiality of mind between Empirical Psychology and Metaphysics. Here again it is possible that, in a changed form, the question whether finite human minds persist when the bodies connected with them are destroyed, may come to be generally admitted as properly within the range of Empirical Psychology, but if so, the method of empirical observation applicable to it will be quite different from ordinary introspective observation.

§ 4. A similar criterion may be applied in drawing the line between Metaphysics and non-metaphysical Philosophy. We may say that so far as the synthesis of the knowable at which Philosophy aims is capable of being verified directly or indirectly by particular experiences, it is *philosophical* but not *metaphysical*. This is the case (*e.g.*) with the Newtonian identification of terrestrial and celestial mechanics, so far as this is verified by the correctness of predictions as to the apparent position of the heavenly bodies; and the same may be said of any similar attempt—whether successful or not—to unite sciences hitherto distinct by reducing their principles and method to common principles and a common method. For instance, the doctrine that the phenomena of life are ultimately explicable by the laws of theoretical physics is philosophical, but not necessarily metaphysical; since if it ever passes from the stage of hypothesis to that of established theory, it will probably be by means of some experiments or observations in which sense-perception has been exercised. And though Philosophy in its widest reach,—*i.e.* when it attempts a synthesis of our knowledge of mind with our knowledge of matter — *generally* becomes metaphysical, this cannot be said to be always the case according to the ordinary usage of the term, and the line above drawn. A co-ordination of the results of empirical psychology with the results of the physical sciences, which shall not involve any propositions incapable of being empirically verified either by introspection or sense-perception, is not only conceivable, but is actually exemplified in a great part of Spencer's Synthetic Philosophy; which, so far as it deals merely with the 'knowable' (so called), is, to a great extent, philosophical, without being what would ordinarily be called metaphysical. I mean so far as it traces, both in the region of matter and in that of mind, a progress from 'indefinite incoherent homogeneity' to 'definite coherent heterogeneity': for these are qualities in which particular states of mind, or groups or successions of such states, may be perceived to resemble particular grouped portions or grouped movements of matter. In fact Mr. Spencer's system seems to me once more to afford a good illustration of the difference between philosophy and metaphysics; for his philosophy of evolution has had a great influence on the thought of the age, and won many disciples; while his metaphysical doctrines, so far as I know, have found few adherents.

I may illustrate this difference still further by

IV THE SCOPE OF METAPHYSICS

referring to a question discussed by Professor Riehl: Is our age a philosophical age?[1] Riehl says that " our scientific age, with its ideas of the indestructibility of energy, of the unitary origin of the forms of life, its explanation of organic processes by the general laws of matter and motion, its connexion of psychology with physiology, is an eminently philosophical age—certainly more philosophical than the age of Schelling's and Hegel's philosophy of nature." I pass over the last phrase, as comparisons are odious when they are not instructive: I have quoted it, not to decide which age is the more philosophical, but to contrast the different character of the two philosophies. The character of Schelling and Hegel's work—even when they dealt with 'philosophy of Nature' was in the main metaphysical; according to my definition. For instance, Hegel told us that 'the moon is the waterless crystal which seeks to complete itself by means of our sea, to quench the thirst of its arid rigidity, and therefore produces ebb and flow.'[2] Now I do not propose to discuss the truth of this remarkable contribution to the theory of the tides. What I wish to point out is that it appears to be clearly incapable of empirical verification, direct or indirect. The alleged effort of the moon to complete itself and quench its thirst has no connection whatever with any part of the system of laws by which physical science explains the empirical facts of terrestrial and celestial motions. On the other hand, the conservation

---

[1] *Der philosophische Kriticismus*, II. ii. p. 84.
[2] Quoted by Riehl, *o.c.* p. 121.

of energy and other principles mentioned by Riehl belong to Philosophy regarded as systematising science, and receive their confirmation entirely from empirical facts: they are not therefore in any degree or manner metaphysical, according to my use of the term.[1]

It seems to me, then, that any study of the world as a whole, which contemplated it from the point of view of the positive sciences—as a world occupying space and changing in time—and which, in its endeavour to put together into a systematic whole the partially systematised knowledge furnished by the aggregate of these sciences, continued to rest on experience as they rest on it, would, according to the usage and tendencies of current thought, be called Philosophy, but *Non - metaphysical* Philosophy. Whereas any study aiming at knowledge of the whole which adopted a different method, discarding verification by particular empirical cognitions, would ultimately fall under the denomination 'Metaphysical.'

To sum up: Metaphysics aims at ascertaining what, if anything, can be known of Matter, Mind, and their relations, besides such knowledge as is based upon or verifiable by particular empirical cognitions: that is, what can be known *à priori* and what can be known

---

[1] But I do not say that all sciences relating to the material world attain their conclusions by inductions from particular experiences: for this would not be admitted by mathematicians generally. Geometry, as we all know, professes to attain its conclusions by deduction from self-evident axioms, combined with definitions of ideal figures, intuitively seen to be possible in space. But however the Geometer's conclusions may be attained, there is no doubt that they are continually verified by their correspondence with empirical measurements.

as necessary or universal elements or conditions of Mind and Cognition.

§ 5. Observe that I say not 'verifiable by experience' but 'verifiable by particular empirical cognitions': I use this phrase because the attempt of a certain school of Philosophy, by the use of a Transcendental Method, to determine the necessary conditions of experience would be affirmed by them to lead to conclusions in a sense verifiable by experience: but in this case the verification is, I conceive, obtained if at all by reflection on any or all experience, not by any particular psychological experiment or observation. Just because it is the necessary conditions of experience which the Transcendentalist seeks to determine, if his theory is not accepted as regards the experience we already possess, it obviously falls altogether: it cannot be left open as a hypothesis possibly verifiable by *other* experiences.

It seems desirable to illustrate this Transcendental Method, of which I have now twice had occasion to speak. I may perhaps illustrate it most conveniently, by explaining briefly the changed relation in which the Metaphysical systems based on it—as compared with older dogmatic Metaphysics—stand to ordinary physical science.

We have seen that the ordinary empirical Physicist turns away from questions as to the beginning in Time of the material world or its extension in Space—whether finite or infinite—and perhaps as to its ultimate constitution. But he turns away from them merely because there is no means of finding an answer to them, not because, if I may so say, there *is* no answer to them in the nature of things. He conceives the material world as a reality which exists independent of his knowledge : which therefore must either have been eternal or have had a beginning in time, must either be infinitely or finitely extended, etc. : although his method of obtaining knowledge does not enable him to decide between the alternatives. Even if he is an Empiricist of a mentalistic or phenomenalistic type, who bases on his Empiricism the conclusion that the real—or the knowable real—is nothing but a series of feelings, he still cannot deny that the question 'when did any series of this kind begin' is one to which there must in the nature of things be some answer if we only knew it. But the Transcendentalist—at least if he is a follower of Kant—discards these questions for a different reason. He holds that Time and Space are not elements of reality, but only forms of the human apprehension of Reality : hence the question, 'When did the past—whether materialistically or mentalistically conceived—really begin,' is to him a futile question, springing from a mere misunderstanding, and is intrinsically as incapable of being answered as the question whether the angles of a triangle are blue or red, heavy or light.

What the Transcendentalist does with Reality, where he brings it to anchor after he has thus floated it 'from out our bourne of Time and Place,' it is beyond my province now to inquire.[1] I merely wished

[1] See Appendix at the end of this lecture.

to illustrate how his conclusions, though based on a study of experience and analysis of its contents, are yet not capable of verification by any particular empirical cognition : for the question whether Time belongs to reality, or only to man's apprehension, as it is a question relating equally to all our experience —which necessarily is or appears to be in time— cannot be decided by the test of any particular experience. The whole application of the Transcendental Method thus belongs to Metaphysics according to the distinctions above drawn, no less than according to usage.

To sum up once more. So far as Metaphysics is concerned with the nature of matter and finite minds, I distinguish it from the positive sciences, Physics and Psychology, and from non-metaphysical Philosophy, primarily by the characteristic that its method dispenses with empirical verification in the sense above explained; and *not* by the characteristic that it studies reality as distinct from appearance : because Physical Science regards its objects as real and itself requires the distinction between Reality and Appearance, and because the objects that Empirical Psychology studies are no doubt transient but not therefore unreal.[1]

---

[1] That is to say the sensations, emotions, thoughts, volitions which it distinguishes, analyses, and classifies, and of which it studies the laws of coexistence and succession, are commonly conceived to be real events in the history of human minds—changes that really happen, not merely appear to happen. So that here again the distinction between Appearance and Reality does not give a generally acceptable line between Psychology and Metaphysics so far as the latter investigates the nature of finite minds.

§ 6. There is another region of inquiry which constructive metaphysicians, from Plato and Aristotle downward, have specially claimed as their own—Rational Theology. For God, considered as the object of metaphysical inquiry, is conceived by all except Agnostics as the One Universal Mind—whatever else may be included in the conception. Here, however, the line that we are called upon to draw in defining Metaphysics is *primâ facie* of a different kind from those already discussed. For theologians generally—at least philosophical theologians—do not hold that it is possible to attain [certain] knowledge of God['s existence] by anything that corresponds to observation and experiment; hence Rational Theology has to be distinguished not from Empirical, but from Revelational Theology.[1]

This distinction, however, I do not propose to examine further till I come to treat of the problem presented by the relation of Theoretical to Practical Philosophy. For it is in the confident solution of this problem which constructive Theology offers that its most obvious interest now lies for educated persons. Were we merely curious to learn what is, has been, and will be, we might be content with Sciences and Positive Philosophy : were we merely desirous of obtaining a clear view of what ought to be, we might be satisfied by an ethico-political system. It is because we require a satisfactory synthesis of these different

---

[1] This, as it stands, too much ignores the teleological view of the physical world, arguments for the existence of God based on evidence of design in organic life, and in the adaptation of organic life to its environment. [To meet this correction of the author's words in brackets are inserted.—ED.]

fundamental conceptions that the offer of Theology, to prove that Good somehow eternally Is, irresistibly claims our attention.

It thus appears that what I described as the 'final and most important' problem of Philosophy—the determination of the relation of 'what is' to 'what ought to be'—belongs to Metaphysics, so far as it is treated in its Theological aspect. But we cannot therefore say that this fundamental problem falls necessarily and entirely within the limits of Metaphysics. For if we give 'good' an empirical interpretation—*e.g.* by defining it as 'desirable feeling or consciousness'—and merely inquire how far 'good' so defined has been or will be realised in the world of living things empirically known, it is obvious that the question will be properly treated by empirical methods. That is, we shall seek the answer to it from Biology, Psychology, and Sociology, and from Philosophy co-ordinating these sciences with Ethics and Politics, without necessarily entering into Theology—or into Metaphysics as we have so far defined it.

§ 7. Returning to the consideration of finite minds and finite matter, we observe that the definition of Metaphysics so far obtained is merely negative. Can we then complete it by adding a positive characteristic? Here I may recur to the view, noticed in the first lecture, that the knowledge which the physical sciences and empirical psychology afford is only knowledge of 'phenomena' or 'appearances,' while at the same time we cannot but believe in the existence of a 'reality underlying appearances,' sometimes referred to as ' the

Absolute.' So far as this view is accepted, it seems in accordance with usage to say that it belongs to **metaphysics** to investigate what may be known of this 'absolute reality,' and the place of the conception of it in a system of rational thought. This statement need not imply that absolute reality can be known: it may be equally accepted, whether the method of Metaphysics is held to lead to positive knowledge of the Absolute, or to be merely critical and limitative, showing that we can only know the 'phenomenal' or the 'relative,'—and perhaps further explaining the origin of the impulse towards knowledge of the Absolute, and even guiding this impulse to some profitable result. It may be accepted (*e.g.*) by Mr. Spencer, who holds that the "reality underlying appearances is totally and for ever inconceivable by us," no less than by Green, who holds that "nature in its reality" implies an eternal "spiritual principle" or "self-distinguishing consciousness," which he calls God. On this view, if we denote systematic knowledge of Reality or Realities—as contrasted with mere Phenomena—by the old name 'Ontology,' we may say that Metaphysics includes Ontology so far as its claims are admitted, and in any case includes an investigation of those claims.

The terms 'absolute' and 'reality,' however, seem to require some further discussion. Sometimes 'the Absolute' is taken to mean that which cannot exist in relation. But this cannot be an object of knowledge, since knowledge is a relation: and it would be absurd to define Metaphysics as the study—from any point of view—of what is *ex vi termini* unknowable. Moreover, if the conception of the Absolute is to have any place at all in our system of thought, it must be conceived in some relation to the phenomena which it 'underlies' or which 'imply' it.

Sometimes, again, the Absolute is understood to be that of which the existence is not limited or conditioned by, or dependent on, the existence of anything other than itself. But—Theology apart—nothing that we know, or have any reason to conceive as possible, can be thought to have this characteristic except the Universe as a whole: and we have no ground for thinking either that the Whole has reality exclusively of its apparent parts, or that its reality should be separately studied. This separation is avoided if we understand the term 'absolute reality' in a third sense, in which it is sometimes used, in antithesis to 'relative,' to denote that which is *completely* real,— *i.e.* that which exists precisely as we apprehend it, independently of its being apprehended by our minds. In this sense, however, we can hardly take it as undisputed that physical science is not concerned with absolute reality; for physical science certainly considers its objects to have the characteristics scientifically attributed to them, independently of their perception by any mind. It is true that physicists are ready to admit, verbally, that they are merely concerned with 'phenomena'; but that would seem to be because any physical fact or event, when scientifically apprehended, is always thought as to some extent different from the same fact as perceived through the senses: accordingly (so far as they are not metaphysicians), the physicists commonly mean by 'phenomenon' not merely 'something that is perceived,' but 'something that happens, *and* is perceived to happen.' As an accepted handbook (Deschanel and Everett) artlessly says, 'A phenomenon is any change that takes place in the condition of a body'; and we cannot advance a step in the explanation of such changes without conceiving bodies to possess permanently certain definite qualities, whether perceived or not.

Here it may be said that Physics is not concerned with the question whether 'matter in itself' really has these qualities, provided it will always consistently appear to have them, as apprehended through the senses; that, in fact, Physics need not trouble itself about the distinction between Reality and completely Consistent Appearance. And this view seems in accordance with the line before drawn between Physics and Metaphysics; since we cannot test by any appeal to particular sense-perceptions the proposition that the whole material world as known through the senses is a mere phenomenon. On the other hand, Physics cannot do without this antithesis of reality and appearance: for it has continually to explain to uninstructed common sense that what really happens is something quite different from what appears to happen: —*e.g.* that our earth moves round the sun; that apparently continuous matter is really composed of discrete parts; that apparently simple matter, as pure water, is really compound. How, then, are its statements in such cases empirically verified? Reflection on this question will, I think, show that the provisional view of 'verification' which I gave at first is inadequate; and that, so far as Physics distinguishes reality and appearance, its criterion is not sense-perception, but consistency with an elaborate and complex system of represented fact, in which the results of many perceptions and inferences are combined according to certain laws. An apparent perception that is inconsistent with this system is declared to be merely apparent; as, *e.g.* when a man 'sees a ghost,' and is afterwards persuaded that he was hallucinated,—because the existence of something so material as to produce through the organ of vision this apparent perception of a man, and yet so immaterial as to pass through the wall of a room, is incompatible with the conception of the physical world, formed by systematising experience. And thus, in another way, we see that the criterion of 'agreement with sense-perception' is inadequate, for it assumes us always to know what is sense-perception, whereas scientific reasoning leads us to conclude that in certain cases what the mind at first takes to be perception through the organs of sense is really a different mental operation.

Indeed, the history of thought shows that the system of conceived reality which thoughtful persons have framed on the basis of particular experiences has varied very much from causes independent of any changes in these experiences. Thus—to take an instance analogous to that of the ghost—Epicurus was not in his age regarded as prone to superstition, but rather as the great deliverer from the terrors of superstition: yet Epicurus held it to be an important argument for the existence of gods that phantasms of them appeared to men in dreams and visions. Again—to take one of the largest changes ever made in our view of the material world—it was not in virtue of any new decisive observations of the heavenly bodies that Copernicus established the heliocentric system of celestial motions: his system prevailed through the greater simplicity and consistency with which it explained phenomena already known.

Further, it is evident that to a great extent our scientific generalisations cannot be verified by any sensible experience; because to a great extent they relate entirely to the past—*e.g.* all that we suppose ourselves to know of the past history of the inorganic world or the world of organic life, or of human society. Now no proposition with regard to the past can be directly verified by sensible experience: so far as we ever regard it as so verified, reflection always shows that we do this on the basis of certain assumptions as to the uniformity of natural laws and causes. Suppose then that any dispute is raised as to the validity of such assumption, how are we to settle it? It does not exactly seem to belong to any physical science to settle it decisively, as the methods characteristic of such sciences seem to be not available for its solution.[1]

[1] Though we cannot, without paradox, as I have shown, draw a line between Physics and Metaphysics by saying that Physics deals with appearance and Metaphysics with reality, we may recognise as an important branch of study that which deals in a comprehensive way with the concep-

Shall we, then, refer the determination of such controversies to Metaphysics or rather to Logic or
tions of Reality, Being, Existence, in their application to the objects of scientific thought.

And it is with this fundamental question that a great part of the historical study called Metaphysics has been concerned.

To the plain man, no doubt, this inquiry seems superfluous in respect of the objects of sense-perception and of Physical Science. The existence of material things as we conceive them—stones, trees, and other objects of experience—seems so clear and certain to him, that it is not easy to get him to take a serious interest in the inquiry, 'How far, and in what sense do these objects really exist with their empirically known qualities, size, weight, colour, structure, life?' Still a little reflection will show not only that the plain man has a view on this question, but also that this view changes and gets involved in perplexity by the progress of Physical Science.

For example, a plain man begins by thinking that material inorganic things are coloured, resonant, etc., quite independently of their relation to any organism. But even the popular science that every educated man learns alters this view; I think, perhaps, most easily as regards sound. For if a plain man asks himself, when he hears one hard body strike another, 'where the sound is'—a very natural and apparently simple question—it does not seem to him (as colour does) to be attached to the colliding hard bodies, but to be coming from them. But when he asks himself what really thus 'comes,' he finds from popular physics that it is vibrations of air, which do not become sound till they reach his ear, and further, from popular physiology, that they do not become sound till they reach his brain: but thus his view of the manner of existence of sound is fundamentally altered.

Still more prominent does this question become when we turn from physical science and its objects to Psychology or Theology. Indeed, it is in reference to these subjects that the need of ontological speculation is most readily perceived. Mankind, even if they feel equal certainty as to the existence of Mind as distinct from a material organism, or as to the existence of God, see that the existence of these objects of thought is not the same in kind as that of material things, or that, at any rate, our knowledge or belief about it is not obtained in the same way; so that there is some difficulty in conceiving and co-ordinating these different manners of existence. An ontological inquiry that shall give us certain and clear convictions in respect of different kinds of existence and their mutual relations is then of real value, if only we can discover the true method of such inquiry.

Now, when the scope of Ontological inquiry is thus made clear, all would agree that it is included in Metaphysics. But whether it constitutes the whole of Metaphysics or a part of it; and, if a part, what part, and what its

Methodology, the general study of method? This question leads us to the fourth and last of the lines that I originally proposed to draw,—viz. that between Metaphysics and Logic or Methodology. This will occupy us in the next lecture.

APPENDIX TO LECTURE IV

TRANSCENDENTALISM AND IDEALISM

THE Transcendentalist holds with the Mentalistic Empiricist or 'Phenomenalist' that Matter as an object of experience is something that we have no ground for regarding as existent apart from experience, since it is composed entirely of *mental* elements. But he holds further that these elements are not to be conceived as really existing, or as having really existed in a series or aggregate of series; since Time and Space, as we have seen, are for him forms of apprehension of the human mind, not elements of the reality of things. When I say that the Transcendentalist holds this, I mean that some part of his language justifies us in attributing to him this opinion: for I seem to find that he is too much under the influence of Common Sense to hold it consistently. But in any case we are justified in regarding as a reasoned conclusion attained by the Transcendental method that of Matter as it exists apart from experience we can know nothing, so completely nothing that the very questions whether it had a beginning or not, is or is not infinitely extended, and what its ultimate parts are, are all alike irrational. For if Time and Space are forms of human sensibility having no application beyond the range of sensible experience, it is illegitimate to carry them beyond this range, even in asking questions.

So much for Matter, how about Mind? Well, Kant

relation is to other parts: and what remains of Metaphysics if we give up as hopeless the inquiry after ontological knowledge—on all these points there is much disagreement, with which I shall deal later.

similarly discards questions as to Mind regarded as a thing in itself. What, according to him, we know in introspection is only how Mind appears to itself. But on the lines of Kantian thought a way out of this 'Agnosticism' was obvious and was soon found. Mind, as a particular substratum of phenomena, was unknowable. But the fundamental assumption of Transcendental Analysis is that the necessary conditions of experience are knowable by analysis of experience; which thus enables us to lay down what thoughts or system of thought is involved in their being an experience at all. Now if knowable these conditions must be in a sense real, though not in Time and Space —Time and Space being among the conditions or forms of sensible apprehension. Thus reflection led to a conception of Thought and the truly Thinkable, as a Reality contrasted with the phenomenal world existing in Time and Space.

And this, in the present state of thought in England, is widely held to be the great object of metaphysical study. The Intellectual Idealists, as I may call them, for distinction—but my term 'Mentalist' allows me to call them simply Idealists—hold that, granting, as we must grant, that Time and Space and the things, material or mental, commonly conceived to exist in Space or in Time or both, are merely phenomenal—mere appearances— there is yet a reality—Eternal Universal Thought—which appears in and through them and may be known by metaphysical study.

And the view that Time and Space do not belong to the world of Real Reality is admitted by Agnostics who profess to know what is out of Time and Space to be unknowable, as well as by Transcendentalists who profess to know much about it. This view is also often admitted by men of science who do not profess to know whether Real Reality is unknowable or not, but are aware that it is unknown to them, and are content to occupy their minds with phenomena.

Now in subsequent lectures I propose to examine this doctrine in the form in which it was held by Green [see Prefatory Note]. But meanwhile it may be convenient that I should give my view of Transcendentalism generally.

1. I am not convinced by the arguments tending to show that Time and Space, Motion and Change are unreal and merely apparent. I admit, however, that there are difficulties in the

conceptions of them, and so far as these difficulties are unsolved, I admit that these objects of thought are imperfectly known, that they would be in some degree altered by complete knowledge. I admit accordingly that it is conceivable that these difficulties would be removed by a thorough grasp of Reality out of Time and Space, not subject to motion or change. If they were removed, we should know exactly how far the current conceptions of Time and Space, and of changes in Time and motions of matter in Space, represented or grasped reality and how far they did not. But until we can somehow transcend the appearance, we cannot know this.

2. For myself, I am unable to form any clear, useful, or definite conception of Reality out of Time and Space: indeed, I can at most suppose that there is such an entity. But it appears to me presumptuous to say that what I do not know is therefore unknowable: and as I find other persons with trained and cultivated intellects consider that they can form a useful conception of this kind of Reality, I am quite disposed to hope that they may be in the right.

3. But speaking for myself and others who find that they cannot grasp this object of Transcendental knowledge, I demand, before I can recognise the inquiry into it as practically legitimate, some proof that knowledge of it will assist us in understanding the so-called phenomenal world. Reality, if known as reality, ought to explain *appearance*. I do not demand that it should explain it completely, but that it should at any rate give *some* help to the understanding of it. Take as analogy the inquiry into space of more than three dimensions. Here again I regard the legitimacy of such an inquiry—from the point of view of a person who can only conceive space of three dimensions—as dependent on its *explanatory utility*. If reasonings about n-dimensional space can be shown to help us to solve problems relating to space of three dimensions, I will admit them as scientific; till this is shown, I regard them as probably idle and fantastic. So with regard to Reality out of Time and Space.

LECTURE V

THE SCOPE OF METAPHYSICS (*continued*)

§ 1. IN seeking for a definition of the subject of Metaphysics, we have still to consider whether it is or is not to include the inquiry which by some thinkers is distinguished from it under the name of Epistemology.

I have taken it to be the business of Philosophy—in Mr. Spencer's words—to 'unify' or systematise as completely as possible our common thought, which it finds partially systematised in a number of different sciences and studies. Now before attempting this unification, we must wish to be somehow assured that the thoughts or beliefs which we seek to systematise completely are true and valid. This is obvious; no rational being with his eyes open would try to work up a mixture of truth and error into a coherent system, without some attempt to eliminate the error.

It is *primâ facie* necessary, therefore, as a preliminary to the task of bringing into—or exhibiting in—coherent relation the different bodies of systematic thought which furnish the matter for Philosophy, to have some criteria for distinguishing truth from error.

It may, however, be thought that this need—though undeniably urgent in the case of such studies as, *e.g.* Politics and Theology—will not be practically presented, so long as the philosopher's work is confined to the positive sciences. The prevalence of error in Politics is kept prominently before our minds by the system of party government; and the effective working of this system almost requires the conviction on either side that the political programme of the other party—unhappily often in a majority—is a tissue of errors. So again in Theology, it is the established belief of average members of any religious denomination that the whole world outside the pale of the denomination lies in the darkness of error on some fundamental points; and even within the pale, the widespread existence of right-hand backslidings and left-hand deflections from the standard of orthodoxy is continually attracting the attention of the newspapers. But, no doubt, in elementary study of the positive sciences error is commonly only brought before our minds in the strictly limited form of slight discrepancy in the results of observation, as something reducible to a minimum by an application of the theory of probabilities.

Still, the danger of error is only thus kept in the background, so long as we confine our attention to the more settled parts of the established sciences in their present condition. Around and beneath these more settled portions, in the region where knowledge is growing in range or depth and the human intellect endeavouring to solve new questions, or penetrate to a more solid basis of principles, we find continually conflict and controversy as to the truth of new conclusions, which appear established and demonstrated to the adventurous minds that have worked them out; and as to the legitimacy of new hypotheses, or the validity of new methods; and wherever we find such conflict and controversy, there must be error on one side or the other, or possibly on both.

Further, as I noticed in speaking of the relation of Philosophy to the Sciences, besides the controversies *within* particular sciences, we also find controversies between different sciences either (1) of a general kind, one science criticising the validity of methods employed by another, or (2) as to particular conclusions. Thus as regards the first, it is at any rate no long time since an important group of physiologists made sweeping attacks on the use of the 'subjective' or 'introspective' method in psychology, which they roundly declared to be incapable of leading to scientific results of any value. As regards special points, I may note a controversy which I understand to be still going on between geologists and physicists as to the past duration of the earth: geologists affirming that their method requires them to claim a longer period than the method of the physicists will allow for the process of bringing our planet into its present condition. Such controversies force on any one who aims at systematising the methods and conclusions of the sciences a searching inquiry into the fundamental assumptions of those methods.

But the fact of scientific error is still more

prominently brought before our minds when we turn from the present to the past, and retrace the history of the now established sciences : since we find that in almost all cases human knowledge has progressed not merely by adding newly ascertained facts to facts previously ascertained, but also, to an important extent, by questioning and correcting or discarding beliefs—often whole systems of connected beliefs—previously held on insufficient grounds. In this way, convinced by Copernicus, the human mind dropped the Ptolemaic astronomy and reconstructed its view of the planetary and celestial motions on the heliocentric hypothesis; convinced by Galileo, it discarded the fundamental errors of Aristotle's view of matter; convinced by Lavoisier, it rectified its conception of chemical elements, and relegated the remarkable substance 'phlogiston'—that had enjoyed an imaginary existence for something like a century—to the limbo of recognised non-entities; convinced by Darwin, it abandoned its fundamental notion of the fixity of organic species, and accepted a revolution in morphological method.

Now the student of science is ordinarily not much disturbed by this evidence that his class forms no exception to Pope's oft-quoted characterisation of man as 'sole judge of truth, in endless error hurled.' When in the progress of thought any prevalent scientific belief is recognised as erroneous, he simply discards this—with more or less endeavour to ascertain the particular causes of error and guard against their recurrence—and, on the whole, continues his usual processes of acquiring, evolving, systematising beliefs with undiminished confidence. But to the philosophical mind the ascertained erroneousness of some beliefs is apt to suggest the possible erroneousness of all. If a belief that I once held to be certainly true has turned out to be false, what guarantees me against a similar discovery in respect of any other belief which I am now holding to be true? The mind is thus overspread with a general and sweeping distrust of the processes of ordinary thinking, which is not exactly to be called philosophical scepticism—since this usually presents itself as systematically deduced from premises accepted by philosophers—but is rather to be conceived as the naïve untechnical scepticism of a philosophic mind, which may turn out to be (as in the classical case of Descartes) a mere stage in its progress toward a dogmatic system. At any rate, it is the removal so far as possible of this philosophic uncertainty—in respect of beliefs that, in ordinary thought, are commonly assumed to be true—that I regard as the primary aim of Epistemology.

So far I have considered only the sciences commonly so-called. But the necessity for the systematic inquiry that I have termed Epistemology becomes still further evident when we consider that there are other more or less systematic studies claiming to be scientific, but not always recognised as such. Philosophy must deal with these claims somehow: and if it takes—as philosophers commonly have taken—the prevalent opinion of educated persons on this question, it must as philosophy be prepared with a rational justification for adopting this criterion of 'real' and 'sham' science. Nor is this opinion always clear and decisive. Not to speak of Psychology, I suppose that Sociology, for instance, is now accepted as a science; but it is not so long since Mr. Leslie Stephen declared that "Sociology at present consists of nothing more than a collection of unverified queries and vague generalities, distinguished under a more or less pretentious apparatus of scientific terminology": and I am not aware that Mr. Stephen has changed his mind.

Then further, we have to consider other studies not commonly called sciences, though too respectable to be regarded as pseudo-sciences, such as Ethics and Theology, which Philosophy must, as we saw, include within its scope. The satisfactory consideration of these in connexion with the positive sciences raises, as is well known, difficulties which cannot, I think, be solved without careful critical examination of the fundamental assumptions and methods, on the one hand, of these studies or branches of knowledge, and, on the other hand, of the positive sciences which are liable to collide with them, and which claim to dominate them. I have said, I trust, enough to show the need of a systematised inquiry into what is taken for knowledge, either universally or by important classes of persons, with the special aim of attaining satisfactory tests of its validity, criteria of its truth and falsehood.

§ 2. Mr. A. J. Balfour defines Philosophy thus: 'Multitudes of propositions, all professing to embody knowledge belonging to one of these three departments [viz. Science, Metaphysics, Ethics], are being continually put forward for our acceptance. And as no one believes all of them, so those who profess to act rationally must hold that there are grounds for rejecting the propositions they disbelieve, and for accepting those they believe. The systematic account of these grounds of belief and disbelief makes up the fourth of the classes into which possible knowledge is divided, and is here always called Philosophy.'[1]

I prefer the more comprehensive definition of Philosophy which I have sought to expound and justify in previous lectures: but I quite admit that the vagueness and variation in the current use of the term gives any thinker a long range of license in selecting the meaning he prefers. And you will observe that Mr. Balfour's view of Philosophy coincides, as far as scope and subject-matter go, with the view previously given, which regards it as concerned with knowledge as a whole, but introduces the limitation of a special end—or rather a special aspect of the end previously overlooked. Philosophy thus understood considers the fundamental principles of all departments of systematic thought, but considers them with the special object of examining their validity and evidence.

For myself, taking, as I have explained, a more comprehensive view of Philosophy, I prefer to distinguish this aspect or function of Philosophy as Epistemology or Theory of knowledge. I call it

[1] *A Defence of Philosophic Doubt*, 1879, pp. 1, 2.

'aspect or function' rather than 'division,' because I do not myself regard the separation between Epistemology and Ontology as other than formal and superficial: for in the main, when we have decided the most important epistemological questions we have, in my view—implicitly though not explicitly—decided the most important ontological questions. Of this more presently. I have now to show that as in the view considered before the difficulty was to distinguish Philosophy from Psychology, so in this latter view the important point is to distinguish it from Logic.

What we primarily want—what Philosophy in this view of it at any rate wants—is a criterion for distinguishing True Beliefs generally from False ones. We all assume that some beliefs are true and others false, and that there is some way or ways of distinguishing the one sort from the other: and the systematic knowledge of these ways is an indispensable element of the systematisation of rational thought, which we have seen to be the function of Philosophy. But Logic is commonly taken to aim at this systematic knowledge, in some measure: the question therefore, how Logic and Epistemology are to be distinguished, is a question requiring careful consideration.

Here, as in other cases which I have examined, we have to admit a considerable variation and uncertainty in common usage: and Logic appears to be sometimes used (*e.g.* by certain Oxford writers, Bradley and Bosanquet) with a scope so extended that it is difficult to find room for any Epistemology outside. But perhaps this is partly due to the comparative recency of the term 'Epistemology' (or even 'Theory of knowledge'); and certainly in the older view of Logic its scope was generally conceived as narrower than that which we have assigned to Epistemology, viz. the systematic investigation of knowledge with the view of making clear the general distinction between truth and error, and the method or methods of applying this distinction successfully in any particular case of alleged knowledge.

§ 3. This more limited view of the sphere of Logic—so far as concerns the criterion of truth—is held by different Schools in modern times though from different points of view. For instance, the Kantian logicians[1] stated it as the function of Pure Logic to give the criterion of *Formal*, but not of *Material* truth. By *Formal Truth* they meant truth as far as it depends on the right use of the faculty of judgment including conception and reasoning, not so far as it depends on the right use of any other faculties, or of anything else that contributes to truth. Whatsoever we conceive, judge, or reason about, they said, we conceive, judge, and reason about, in the same way, at any rate if our thought is really to be called thought: that is, as they said, reasoning or thought deserving the name has the same *form*, though its *matter* varies as we pass from one subject to another. Logic then examines the form of our conceptions, judgments, and reasonings about things, and in so far as errors can be shown to lie in this form points out and puts us on our guard against such error. Thus if

[1] *E.g.* Mansel, *Prolegomena Logica*.

a complex conception contains contradictory elements, or if a proposition is a 'contradiction in terms,' that is, denies what is a part of the meaning of the subject, or if a piece of reasoning, when thrown into a syllogistic form, is such that the conclusion does not necessarily follow from the premises—the thought in question is formally bad. Logic, thus, it is said, secures us formal correctness in our judgments. But why does it not secure material truth? The answer that the Kantian school usually gave to this question is that *any general criterion of material truth is impossible*: material truth varying in its nature with the variety of objects about which we think.

§ 4. Mill's position is somewhat different: he treats the distinction between Formal and Material truth as a useless subtlety; but he limits Logic much in the same way as the Kantians, though not from the same point of view. Logic he regards as giving a criterion of truth so far as it depends on *inference*, but manifest incorrectness — of the kind above illustrated—in the form of conceptions and judgments taken by themselves, he thought, hardly ever occurs. It is true that another kind of formal defect in our conceptions and judgments as expressed in language —vagueness, indefiniteness, and ambiguity—is continually occurring: but in order to remedy this kind of defect we have for the most part to consider the matter of discourse, and to go beyond the scope of Formal Logic. Pure Logic does not profess to remove verbal ambiguities, except in its own words—such as 'some,' 'or.' We have now, however, to observe that

Mill does not altogether confine his discourse to inferred judgments. And an examination of his actual procedure in this respect will bring us back to the point from which I digressed at the outset of the lecture,—the relation of Metaphysics to Logic. For there are *primâ facie* two kinds of propositions the truth of which Mill's Logic does not profess to secure: (1) Particular propositions obtained by direct observation and not by inference, and (2) General propositions obtained by direct intuition and not by inference. And accordingly the discussion of the existence of Truth and Falsehood in the case of both of these is by Mill formally relegated to another science, viz. Metaphysics. "The grand question," he says, "of what is called metaphysics is, What are the propositions which may reasonably be received without proof?" (*Log.* v. c. iii. § 1). That is, just as Logic gives the criteria of true inferences, or truths mediately known, so Metaphysics gives the criteria of true perceptions or intuitions, truths immediately known; so that the two together make up a complete investigation of the general characteristics or criteria of truth.

But this reference of such questions to Metaphysics is found to be illusory with regard to general propositions at least; as it is sufficiently evident that, in Mill's view, their truth is really inferential, that is, depends on correct induction. This is partly made clear in the long discussions in Book II. on 'Necessary Truths or Axioms' (chaps. v.-vii.); and, later, when he comes to treat Fallacies, Mill makes a clean sweep of the *a priori* assumptions of various antecedent philosophers, under the head of 'Fallacies of simple inspection,' or '*a priori* fallacies' (cf. bk. v. chap. iii.). Again, turning to particular observations, we find that Mill (in bk. iv. chap. i., 'Observation and Inference,' supplemented by bk. v. chap. iv., 'Fallacies of Observation') does at least partially enter into the question of the sources of error and the means of avoiding error, not in the process of inductive reasoning, but in the 'observation' which supplies us with the particular premises of such reasonings.

In short we find that, both as regards the particular premises of scientific reasoning which we call 'observed facts,' and the universal premises—whether intuitions or fundamental assumptions—Mill's Logic continually overlaps the narrower limits that he has drawn for it, and becomes a general theory of the criteria of truth, enters in fact on that other portion of Epistemology which he seems to have relegated to Metaphysics.

General Logic, or Methodology, and Metaphysics (as conceived by Mill) are two closely connected departments, it seems to me, of a general theory of evidence or philosophical certitude. Hence though we thus have Mill's authority for defining Metaphysics so as to include the portion of Epistemology which his definition of Logic expressly leaves on one side, we must be on our guard against aiming at too decisive a separation between the two.

Just as an inquiry like Mill's, which concentrates attention primarily on the Theory of Valid Inference, finds it practically impossible to exclude the question of the validity of propositions obtained—by those who hold them—otherwise than by inference; so Epistemology, concentrating attention primarily on the latter question, cannot wholly leave on one side the theory of valid inference. It will have nothing to say on many topics which ordinary Logic treats in systematic detail: on syllogistic moods and figures and reductions of syllogisms, for example; and not much on the four or more Methods of Induction which Mill puts forward. But in examining the validity of the fundamental conceptions and intuitions or assumptions of Science or Ontology, it will be compelled also to study in some measure the processes of mediate thought which employ these conceptions and, resting on these intuitions or assumptions, attain conclusions of philosophical importance: though it should try to keep this study of Inference as strictly philosophical and as little technically logical as possible.

§ 5. The question then is, how far such a theory of evidence, including self-evidence, is properly connected with Metaphysics as previously defined. My view is that provisionally at least—so long as the procedure of Metaphysics is as uncertain and controverted as it is at present—this connexion is inevitable. The 'investigation of the claims of Ontology' of which I spoke must form part of a general theory of the criteria for distinguishing truth from error: indeed the distinction between 'reality' and 'appearance' can hardly be studied separately from the distinction between 'truth' and 'error': since truth, so far as it relates to what is, has been, or will be, is the representation of reality in thought expressible in words. It would, indeed, be paradoxical to affirm that *all* truth has this direct relation to actual existence; since the distinction between truth and error is commonly held to be applicable to propositions relating to what ought to be, and also to affirmations as to the logical connexion of merely hypothetical premises and conclusions. If therefore the claims of Ontology should ever come to be incontrovertibly established, and its method should come to be as fixed and accepted as the methods of the physical sciences are, it may perhaps then be thought more proper to separate Epistemology or Methodology from Ontology, no less than from Physics. At present, it seems best that the general investigation of the grounds of our belief in such conclusions as are held to be based on experience should be combined with the study of what may be known, or has been thought to be known, by a non-empirical method about mind, matter, and their relations, or about the 'absolute reality' that 'underlies' or is 'implied in' the world empirically known: especially since, as we have seen, the notion of 'verification by experience' appears to be inadequately analysed and defined in ordinary thought. And I conceive it is in accordance with usage to give to this investigation as a whole the name of Metaphysics.

APPENDIX TO LECTURE V

RELATION OF EPISTEMOLOGY TO ONTOLOGY

To show the difficulty of separating Epistemology from Ontology I may refer to Külpe's third epistemological controversy as to Idealism, Realism, and Phenomenalism. I cannot conceive how the issues raised by this controversy can be regarded as other than Metaphysical in Külpe's sense.

First, it will be observed that Külpe brings the antithesis between Idealism and Realism under the head of Epistemology as distinguished from Metaphysics in the narrower sense of Ontology. Further, he conceives Epistemology to be concerned with three questions : (1) as to the origin of knowledge, (2) as to its validity or limitations, (3) as to the nature of its objects or contents. According to my view the second is the primary epistemological question. Epistemology is concerned with the first question only so far as that is connected with this [1]; and when we come to (3) any separation between Epistemology and Metaphysics or Ontology becomes forced and perplexing rather than helpful. For *primâ facie* the object of Knowledge is Being, 'what is': when we truly know a thing we believe that it really is what we perceive or think it to be. Thus any general theory of the nature of the object of knowledge cannot properly be divided from a general view as to the nature of Being.

Külpe no doubt tries to avoid this in his definition of Idealism: "Idealism maintains that everything knowable ... is in its proper and original nature simply content of consciousness" (§ 26, p. 194). This seems to leave it doubtful whether there

---

[1] Empiricism in Epistemology is, according to me, not the view that experience is the origin of our ideas, but the view that particular cognitions are alone ultimately valid as premises of scientific reasoning, and universal propositions only valid so far as they are based on these. Accordingly the Rationalism which I oppose to it is the view that affirms the validity of intuitive cognitions universal in form, if in abstract reflection—a process referred to Reason—they are clearly and distinctly seen to be true.

is anything besides consciousness; and in fact Külpe expressly declares that epistemology is not competent to decide concerning *existence*. It is, of course, possible to hold that all that is knowable consists of ideas or data of consciousness and yet to leave the question of existence undecided. But it seems to me more in accordance with usage to call this Phenomenalism or Positivism rather than Idealism.

Külpe's definition of Realism is less guarded and appears frankly ontological. "The characteristic of Realism," he says, "consists in the recognition of an external world existing independently of the ideas or states of consciousness of the knowing subject." The antithesis of Idealism and Realism as defined by Külpe then turns on the opposition between *idea* and *fact*, between what is merely imagined or thought and what 'exists in reality.' But we observe that this distinction, as applied in ordinary thought, is applicable to the contents of consciousness no less than to facts of the material world. My idea of what another thinks and feels may be very unlike what he *really* thinks and feels; and this unlikeness is continually brought before our notice by the experience of life. The opposition of Realism and Idealism as explained by Külpe is again a bad opposition, because it suggests that states of consciousness are not real: but the plain modern man does not think this, though the materialist may. I use *Dualism*, therefore, not Realism, to express what Külpe here defines as Realism. And when we note that Külpe himself describes Dualism as looking upon "matter and mind, the subjective and the objective, as two separate and independent existences" (§ 18, p. 133), it surely becomes difficult to distinguish between this and what he calls Realism; and we are led to seek some explanation of this double characterisation of what seems broadly the same view— the view that matter exists independently of mind.[1]

---

[1] The explanation is, I think, to be found in that double relation of Mind to matter noticed in the third lecture (Relation of Philosophy to Psychology). In our ordinary view of the empirical world and its process, as I pointed out, Mind *quâ* Cognitive is tied to Matter at two ends: not only is some material process (in the grey matter of the brain) the invariable accompaniment of every mental process: but at the same time the mental process may be a cognition of matter.

Now in discussing Dualism Külpe has the former relation *primarily* in view; his question is whether we can regard these psychophysical 'two-sided' processes in the brain, taken along with their physical causes and effects, as due to the 'interaction' of two distinct substances. He says (p. 135) that "the standpoint is generally discredited as inadequate to the problem of interaction," and in arguing the *pros* and *cons* of Dualism, he considers it as opposed to Materialism and what I venture to call Materialistic Monism, the view that regards the mental fact—thought and feeling—as an appearance of or mysterious appendage to the material process in the brain.

But when he comes to Realism, he has the other antithesis in view—the relation of matter to mind as an object of perception ; and therefore primarily of matter external to the organism (not the grey matter of the brain). Here the opposition is not to Materialism or Materialistic Monism, but to Idealism or what I call Mentalism.

LECTURE VI

RELATION OF PHILOSOPHY TO HISTORY

§ 1. In the preceding lectures my aim has been to define the Scope of Philosophy neutrally—*i.e.* so as to avoid adapting it only to the view of any one philosophical school, on points that are still matter of controversy. With this aim, I was led ultimately to define it as the study in which the principles, methods, and main conclusions of the special sciences and other departments of systematic thought are compared and considered together, with the view of reducing them, as far as possible, to a higher unity of system. In the process of attaining and making clear this definition, I considered the relation of Philosophy to the physical sciences, to ethics and politics, to psychology and, briefly, to logic and methodology. I also took pains to make clear the relation of the wider term Philosophy to the narrower term Metaphysics, which evidently denotes a part or kind of Philosophy. But there is one ancient and important study which I did not mention in this connexion, namely, History.

One reason for this omission was that the relation of Philosophy to History is, in the present state of thought, somewhat obscured and perplexed by various differences and confusions of meaning, and in trying to dispel this confusion we are inevitably led to consider the relation of Philosophy to Sociology: this I also thought it best to defer, as entailing a peculiarly complicated and prolonged discussion.

To these two closely connected questions I now propose to pass. I begin by noticing a remarkable change of view as to the relation of Philosophy to History, causing some confusion. According to the older view of History, taking the term in its widest sense so as to include Natural as well as Human History, it is the business of History to ascertain particular facts; Science then systematises the results of History, by ascertaining relations of resemblance and empirical laws or general relations of sequence and co-existence among these particular facts: finally comes Philosophy, which systematises the results of science. History, thus viewed, is at the bottom of the scale of knowledge, conceived as rising from the particular to the general; nearest to the particularity of empirical fact, and furthest from the unity of thought at which Philosophy aims.

This is, as I say, the ancient view of History, but there are many signs that this view is now not only ancient but antiquated. The nineteenth century has been called, in contrast with the eighteenth, a pre-eminently historical century—the eighteenth being the 'Seculum Rationalisticum'—and in the energetic and continuous progress which the study of history has certainly exhibited in the century drawing to a close, it has developed a strong tendency not to be content with the humble position above assigned to it. It has brought to the front the conception of a 'Historical Method,' conceived not merely as the right method of studying history, but as the right method of studying other subjects. Indeed, in the view of its enthusiastic admirers, it seems to be held the right method of studying *all* other subjects; for it is claimed that it has 'invaded and transformed all departments of thought.' But if this be so, it concerns philosophy much to examine the nature and extent of this invasion and transformation; for if this breadth of scope, and this height of pretension be admitted, it seems at least doubtful whether the Historical Method can leave room for any important and effective philosophical method distinct and apart from it. It is true that some of the most eager advocates of the Historical Method take pains to explain that they not only leave room for Philosophy, but even concede the first rank to it, as the more dignified and profound inquiry: they confine themselves merely to the relative and phenomenal, and—with the utmost formal courtesy and humility—leave the whole sphere of Absolute Being for philosophy to study. But this humility and courtesy is usually ironical: the Absolute thus left is usually held to be unknowable; the egg thus offered for simple-minded philosophy to brood over is shrewdly suspected of being addled. At any rate if we are to admit the claims of the Historical Method, in all the breadth and fulness with which they are widely asserted, we shall have to admit that it constitutes an indispensable and main part of philosophical method so far as Philosophy is concerned with objects of knowledge other than Absolute Being. Now I do not for a moment deny the interest and importance of studying the past, with a view to the understanding of the present and future, in any department of the world of changing things and events which constitutes ·the object of empirical knowledge. But I think that the dominant and architectonic position which is now sometimes claimed for this study of the past is claimed unwarrantably, with an exaggeration due to confusion of thought. In order to make this clear, I propose in the first instance to take history to include the study of past changes, whether of things or thoughts. It is, indeed, the history of human thoughts about things which primarily concerns us, in considering the relation of Philosophy to History and the so-called 'Historical Method': but, for reasons that will appear hereafter, I think that a brief consideration of the wider question will be a useful preliminary to the discussion of the narrower.

I must begin, however, by limiting somewhat the temporal meaning of History :—or rather by expressing a limitation which it is usual to make tacitly in discussing the subject. History, in the sense in which 'Natural History' is a species of it, includes all recorded facts : all the facts on which the generalisations of any empirical science are based are at the present moment 'portions and parcels of the dreadful past' in the sense that they were observed and recorded in past time. But if we were to take History in this widest meaning, the historical method could hardly be distinguished from the inductive method; and its alleged 'invasion' would not mean more than a spread of a tendency in all departments of thought to pay more attention to facts and less to deductive reasoning from general premises, assumed or supposed to be self-evident. Well, no doubt this movement is to some extent real, at least in departments that I know about. The German of fable, who sat down to evolve a camel out of his inner consciousness, was certainly not a Teuton up to date: we cannot place him later than the first half of the century. Of course I need hardly say that even this old-time German never evolved out of his inner consciousness anything so insignificant as a camel: but he might have been capable of evolving the principles of chemistry or the proper constitution of the Modern State. But what has happened to this mythical Teuton, and the relation of induction to deduction in science generally—this is beyond the scope of my present inquiry.

In the present discussion, then, I propose to take History in the ordinary sense of the more or less distant past: the past so far as we can trace it back. For the Historical Method which is supposed to have invaded and transformed all departments of thought is mainly the method of studying the more or less remote past, so far as it is different from the *recent* past:—it is a method of studying in each department the whole series of changes either in things thought about or our thoughts about them, in order to understand the general laws of these changes and so comprehend and explain the present as resulting from the past in accordance with these laws. It is the claims of History thus regarded, as presenting not merely facts in chronological order, but laws of development, which I propose to examine not in a hostile, but in a critical spirit.

§ 2. Let us take, then, in order the chief departments of science, and consider briefly how far it is true that they have been 'invaded' by the Historical Method, distinguishing the two cases I have brought together—viz. the past history of things or objects, and the past history of thoughts.

As regards the former, it is obvious that no such invasion has taken place, or is threatened, in the department of pure mathematics—the sciences of space, number, abstract quantity. The objects of these sciences, the relations which they investigate are, of course, independent of time: they cannot be conceived as having had a past different from the present. Our conceptions of these relations have had a history no doubt; and in the general increase of historic interest, which is characteristic of our age, this branch of historic inquiry has, among others, received its share of attention. But whatever philosophic aim the students of the past history of mathematics may propose to themselves, they certainly do not propose to modify the received method of mathematical reasoning by the introduction of a historical element; or to support the fundamental assumptions of mathematics by arguments drawn from history; or to explain anything that may seem unexplained or arbitrary in these assumptions by a reference to the process of development through which they have passed.

Much the same may be said of the fundamental universal premises which we use in our general reasonings about the material world—the laws of motion, or the law of gravitation. We conceive such laws to have operated unchanged through all conceivable time; and whatever doubts and disputes may exist either as to the exact way in which such laws should be formulated or the exact nature of the evidence on which they rest, we do not commonly suppose that this doubt and conflict admit of being solved by any knowledge of the process of development through which our conceptions have come to be what they are. This applies both to Mechanics regarded as a special science, and to Mechanics widened into Natural Philosophy, into an attempt, that is to say, to explain all physical phenomena by dynamical principles. Whatever need we feel of further light on the fundamental notions of mass and conservation of mass; on energy and conservation of energy; on the ultimate constitution of matter, molecular and atomic; on the laws of molecular motion, and their relation to the laws of chemical combination, etc.,—we do not commonly expect to get this light by looking backwards; but either by reflecting more carefully and profoundly on the facts provisionally systematised and our present conceptions of these, or by looking more carefully, with the present resources of experiment and observation, at the world as it is here and now before us; or rather by both processes combined.

It seems to me, therefore, that the methods and conclusions of mathematics and rational physics cannot be materially affected by the historical method. In order to establish this decisively, I have allowed myself briefly to consider together in reference to these sciences both applications of the historical method— the application to *things* as well as that to *thoughts*. In the rest of the present discussion I shall, for clearness, confine myself to the history of fact, leaving the history of thought, on the subjects to which I shall now proceed, for a subsequent lecture.

For what I have said of the complete exclusion of the historical method from rational physics as an abstract science is, I admit, no longer applicable when we contemplate the physical universe as a particular concrete fact and seek for an explanation of its concreteness and particularity: when we ask why there should be seventy or more different kinds of matter distributed in what appears to be so arbitrary and irregular a manner through the spherical mass on which we are carried about in space, and why there should be—as astronomy declares—a no less apparently irregular and arbitrary distribution of this or other matter through the rest of space. Here no doubt we have a problem for which some inquiring minds have sought a solution in history—in the wide sense in which I am now using the term: they have hoped, by studying the processes of change through which the physical universe has passed, to find some explanation of the complex of irregular differences which its actual condition exhibits. And it may be fairly claimed that—in the wider sense which we are now giving to history—the nebular theory does connect astronomy and geology and physics into one historical study of the knowable physical universe as a complex, concrete fact.

I should not think of denying the interest and importance of this speculative physical history, nor am I competent to criticise the methods by which it has been worked out. But I venture to affirm that whatever success may have been obtained in tracing back the past states of the physical universe has not really helped us a step towards a philosophical solution of this problem: all that has been done is to change one particular mode of arbitrariness and irregularity for another no less apparently unaccountable.

This negative result, indeed, is not always plain at first sight. For example, when we first consider the formula in which Mr. Spencer generalises the process through which the physical universe has passed, and contemplates matter "passing from an indefinite, incoherent homogeneity to a definite, coherent heterogeneity," it seems at first sight that our complex of arbitrary differences might be ultimately simplified away if we could retrace this process far enough back. But reflection shows that the 'indefiniteness' which Mr. Spencer attributes to primæval matter is not a condition of matter as we conceive it to have existed, but only relates to its apprehension by our limited intellects. If we conceive any particle of matter as existing at all, we of necessity conceive its spatial and kinematic relations as perfectly definite. Similarly, we are forced to conceive every particle of matter as always in a sense coherent—that is, connected by dynamic relations—with every other particle. The discovery of the law of gravitation at once and permanently introduced this degree of definiteness into our conception of the physical universe. And finally, whatever heterogeneity the whole aggregate now possesses requires us to suppose a corresponding heterogeneity at every point of the process of complex motion through which it has passed in time. I say 'a corresponding,' not 'an equal' heterogeneity, because I quite admit that, in the earliest stage to which the nebular hypothesis takes us back, it leads us to conceive matter as more uniformly distributed through space. The process which Mr. Spencer describes as a process from the homogeneous to the heterogeneous is a process which may increase the *amount* of difference between the parts of space compared, in respect of their occupation by matter; but it is not a process which can *originate* any difference, it can only reduce the size of the parts of space between which the difference exists. The heterogeneity that now exists between larger parts of space in the whole space through which our planetary system extends:—*e.g.* the difference between the space occupied by our planet with its atmosphere and any equal and similar contiguous portion of space—this heterogeneity no doubt seems to disappear when we have, in idea, resolved the whole aggregate of planets into a continuous rotating nebula. But this appearance is merely due to the fact that we happen to concentrate attention on the interplanetary spaces: in truth the heterogeneity has not disappeared, it has only been broken up smaller. The differences that are now found in the comparison of parts of space as large as planets were then only to be found by comparing parts of space of the size of molecules and atoms. With whatever confidence we may give the rein to the most audacious of speculative astronomers, and under his guidance sweep back through æons of time to the most diffused of nebulæ, we shall yet find in the nebula with which we leave off a complex of apparently arbitrary and irregular differences, needing explanation just as much—or just as little—as the particularities of our actual planet, rolling in the 'gleam of a million millions of suns.'

In saying this, I must repeat that I do not mean in any way to depreciate the interest and importance of attempts to trace out the past history of the cosmos, by speculative geology and speculative astronomy combined: I wish merely to point out that, whatever degree of success may crown such efforts, there is no prospect that they will tend to solve the philosophical problem suggested by the actual particularity of the cosmos. If we take as given—as our point of departure—the positions and velocities of all parts of the physical world at any point of time, present or past, we may reasonably regard all subsequent changes as ultimately explicable by the known laws of physical motion, and the partially known laws of chemical combination. If we take any two such points of time —say the present and the remotest past to which the most daring hypothesis can carry us back—we can reasonably regard the intervening changes as thus explicable. But however far back we go, the state of matter at the point of time that we began with is exactly as inexplicable as the state of matter now: it presents the same unsolved problem to Philosophy, which aims at an explanation of the world as a whole. And this being so, any conjectural history of the past which we construct—however valid the reasoning on which it is based—will not in any way affect the received methods of rational physics or natural philosophy: nor do I see how it is likely to affect the received methods of chemistry.

§ 3. But what shall we say of the sciences that deal with organic life? Is it not true that zoology and botany have been 'invaded and transformed' by the Darwinian theory, and all the speculation and investigation about the development of organic life to which it has given rise? It is certainly true that this historical biology—if I may be allowed the term —has wrought a change in our general conception of the actual differences in the organic world, to which no parallel can be found in the sciences dealing with inorganic matter. For no hypothetical history that has been offered us of the inorganic world has even professed to explain how the qualitative differences have arisen—the differences in *kinds* of matter—which modern chemistry still presents to us as unreduced: at least it has not professed to explain them by any method resting on an empirical basis and capable of being tested by facts. Whereas the hypothetical history of the organic world which we owe to Darwin does attempt to show how differences of kind, in the matter with which it deals, have been developed out of an original homogeneity.

If the Darwinian theory, in its broad outlines, is valid, we may reasonably suppose that the world of living things was—at a point of time much less remote than that to which the nebular hypothesis carries us back—far more homogeneous than it now is: the source of the greater heterogeneity which the later time shows lying primarily in the indirect action of the diverse inorganic environment on different parts of this world of living things. Differences in external relations, in the situations and circumstances of living things have thus, in the course of ages, been taken in—if I may so say—and transformed into differences of internal relations, differences of organisation.

It is therefore in a sense true that the historical or evolutional method of biology has 'transformed' previously existing departments of knowledge; at any rate it has annexed to science a new and important region hitherto desolate and only viewed as it were from a sort of philosophic Pisgah as possibly destined for orderly scientific cultivation. The Darwinian theory has opened out to us an entirely new view full of interesting detail, of the meaning and import of relations among living things—and between living things and their environment—which were always there to observe, though often overlooked—*e.g.* the curious resemblances between species of plants or animals, often of very different genera, through which one species escapes the attacks of certain enemies by looking like another species which these enemies do not attack.

Still though our knowledge of the world of life has thus become more full and penetrating, whatever positive systematic knowledge of living things was thought to be given us by zoology and botany, pursued on pre-Darwinian methods, is in no way invalidated or set aside by the newer speculations : what has been invalidated is merely the negative conception of ultimate irreducibility as regards specific and generic differences. And it is important to observe that even an elementary knowledge of the history of life on this planet combined with a philosophical grasp of the present conditions of life had made the popular conception of ultimately irreducible differences of kind philosophically untenable, before Darwin's theory was produced; for it had become evident from the geological record that we could not deal with organic as with inorganic differences of kind, by throwing them back to the inscrutable origin of all things. Our existing fauna and flora must be held to have appeared on the planet after long periods of time, in which pre-existing species had lived and died out: they could not have trooped in, as we know them, on the most conveniently arranged fleet of meteors : they must therefore have come into being on the planet: but how? 'Special Creation' was a popular answer; but, scientifically considered, special creation was a purely negative notion: it simply denied a causal relation, in the sense in which empirical science understands the term causal, between the novel fact, the newly existing species, and all antecedent cosmical facts: and no philosopher could accept such a denial, at least without evidence which can hardly be conceived and certainly could not be produced. But if the new organism was not, physically speaking, uncaused, its production must be due either to conditions of pre-existing inorganic matter, or to other organic life: these were the only two alternatives, and of the two the latter was indefinitely more probable even before we had any evidence from which we could infer the particular nature of this causal connexion.

It has always struck me that in the active, and sometimes heated, discussion which took place a generation ago, on Darwinism and Evolution, the philosophical reasons for accepting the general conception of biological Evolution were not sufficiently distinguished from the scientific reasons for accepting the Darwinian theory. This was not unnatural, because no doubt the new conceptions of 'struggle for existence' and 'survival of the fittest' and the detailed evidence of the widespread operation of the causes of change in living forms which these conceptions represented, did in fact greatly contribute to the force of the philosophical arguments against what may be called 'Creationism.' At the same time, it is important to recognise that the two lines of argument are quite distinct: and it is quite possible to accept the general doctrines of the historical continuity of life and the derivation of all living things from antecedent living things, without holding that we have adequate grounds for regarding the Darwinian—or any other—theory of the mode and process of derivation as giving a complete explanation of the facts.

This point is important to us on account of the great influence which the conceptions of Biology, and especially the evolutionary method in Biology, has had upon the development of Sociology. For in Sociology the general conception of evolution, of the gradual and continuous growth of new forms of polity and social relations out of old forms, has been commonly accepted without question from the first;[1] but the application of the notions of struggle for existence and survival of the fittest is much more doubtful and disputed. But keeping now to Biology, it may be said that whether, on the one hand, we simply contemplate the general theory of biological evolution and the philosophical reasons in its favour, or, on the other, accept the special Darwinian doctrine of the struggle for existence and the survival of the fittest as the leading or sole factor in causing changes in forms of life—it remains equally undeniable that the study of Biology has been invaded and transformed

[1] What corresponds to Creationism here is the attribution of novelties to heroes, men of genius, etc.

by an evolutionary and in a wide sense historical method. And I do not deny it; but I wish to point out that if, on the one hand, all this is true, it is no less true that our theory of past change has been determined by our scientific knowledge based on observation and experiment of changes actually taking place. If the past of life taken as a whole helps us to comprehend the present, it is only on the assumption that the past, so far as we venture to trace it back, has been in essentials like the present; and that no causes have operated to produce morphological changes in the past, except those which we know to have operated in times quite recent.

Let us take first the philosophical argument. Why do we reject the doctrine of 'Special Creation' when put forward as an alternative to Evolution, in respect—let us say—of the coming into being of the type of animal known as *Plesiosaurus?* Because, firstly, it is an assumption on which the whole of our *actual* investigation of the physical world depends that all changes have physical causes, and we have no positive reasons to set against this assumption in the case supposed: and because, secondly, if we admit that the coming into being of the *Plesiosaurus* was a physical event or complex of events causally connected with physical antecedents, it is in accordance with *recent* experience scientifically investigated to assume the animal to have come into being through biogenesis and not through abiogenesis.

So again, if we accept the Darwinian theory as giving an adequate account of the specific process of evolution—rejecting the Lamarckian (*direct* modification by the environment)—it is because we hold that recent experience scientifically investigated shows the influence of the environment on organic forms through the struggle for existence and survival of the fittest to be a cause really operative, and that we have no clear evidence of any other cause. In either case our view of the remote past is altogether determined by the conclusions formed from scientific study of the present and recent past. And therefore even this splendid triumph of what may be called, in a wide sense, historical study turns out to be an example of the paramount importance of the study of the present in determining the basis on which we interpret the records of the past; rather than of the paramount importance of the study of the past, in determining the scientific principles on which we frame our conception of the present.

LECTURE VII

RELATION OF PHILOSOPHY TO HISTORY (*continued*)

§ 1. IN my last lecture I was occupied in considering the relation of Philosophy to History: and especially— taking History at once in its widest range and deepest interpretation, as a study of the past, pursued with a view of ascertaining laws of change and development —the recent claim of History to supply a universal and dominant method to all studies. I examined this claim in relation to the sciences that are concerned with the inorganic world, distinguishing between the recent past and the remote past in order to obtain a clear issue, and a clear distinction between the Historical Method and the Inductive Method. I pointed out first that Mathematics and Abstract Physics were obviously unaffected by the Historical Method: meaning by Abstract Physics the study of the general laws of matter and motion, as distinct from the study of the particularities of the concrete physical universe in which we find ourselves placed. It is no doubt true, when we turn to Concrete Physics, that we find a very interesting, though highly speculative branch of History—in the wide sense of a study of the past—which, based upon and combining Astronomy and Geology, professes to explain how the Solar System, as we know it, was developed out of an original rotating nebula. Without denying the interest of this hypothetical history, I pointed out that its explanatory force was liable to be exaggerated: since however far, and within whatever degree of probability, we can trace back the antecedent conditions in time of the physical universe, the particular collocations of material particles at the point at which we leave off present a philosophical problem requiring just as much explanation as the actual physical world in which we now live. We do not really get back, even with the utmost aid from conjecture, from heterogeneity to homogeneity.

The case is different, no doubt, when we turn to the hypothetical history of the world of organic life, which has become current under the influence of Darwin's work. So far as we accept this theory of Biological Evolution, it does show us how the differences of kind in living things have been developed, in continually increasing magnitude and complexity, from an originally simpler and more homogeneous condition of life, through the influence, direct or indirect, of the differences in the environment. And undoubtedly the view thus formed of the past history of living things profoundly modifies our view of their actually existing differences, by explaining the manner in which these have been developed. But I pointed out that if a study of the Past of life, taken as a whole, thus helps us to comprehend the Present, it is equally true that this is because our method of studying the recent past is based upon our scientific knowledge of the present, and assumes that the causes which have operated to produce morphological changes in the past are the same as those which we know to have operated in recent times, subjected to scientific observation and experiment. And therefore I think the new history of organic life which the Darwinian theory gave us, so far from invalidating anything that we had before taken for positive knowledge of living beings, did not even meet, in philosophically trained minds, with any prepossessions that had to be overthrown.

§ 2. It may be thought, however, that — even granting what I have just urged to be true of the study of organic life generally—it cannot be true of the living being that interests us more than all the rest, of man. Surely, it may be said, if we admit that man has been gradually developed out of an ascidian or other low organism, the old conception of a dual nature of man, a mysterious combination of spirit and body, will have to be given up: materialism then clearly wins in its old conflict with spiritualism. I know that this is a popular inference from the Darwinian theory; but I cannot see that it has any philosophical basis. However completely we accept the theory, all the really philosophical obstacles in the way of a purely materialistic view of man appear to me to remain unchanged. It remains true, as Mr. Spencer says—and the statement is perhaps more impressive as coming from him than if made by a more idealistic philosopher — it remains true that psychical facts, as known to us by 'subjective observation and analysis,' have no 'perceptible or conceivable community of nature' with physical facts, ascertained by objective observation and analysis: it remains true that—as the same writer says—"of the two it seems easier to translate so-called matter into so-called spirit, than to translate so-called spirit into so-called matter (which latter is, indeed, wholly impossible)."[1]

It may be replied that even granting the untenability of mere materialism, the Darwinian theory of the origin of man renders it impossible for us to conceive of the continued existence of the individual man after his physical death; and that therefore, however the metaphysical issue between materialism and idealism may be settled or left unsettled, at any rate Evolution has eliminated the old belief in the immortality of the soul; so that materialism wins on the only point of any practical importance to a plain man.

If historical biology had achieved this result, I should recognise that it had 'invaded' with tremendous effect our study of man and his destiny; but the supposed achievement appears to me quite illusory. To show this let us consider briefly what grounds there are, apart from the Darwinian theory, for coming to a philosophical conclusion on the fundamental question—Does the individual mind result from a certain organisation of an individual organism, and

[1] *Principles of Psychology*, §§ 41, 63.

terminate when the organisation is destroyed?—admitting that here, in the view of common sense, almost the whole interest of metaphysics is concentrated; that the metaphysician's 'Yes' or 'No' or 'Not proven,' in answer to this question, is, for the plain man, *der langen Rede kurzer Sinn.*

In order to ascertain how far historical biology throws any light on this question, let us briefly survey the chief considerations that incline us to answer it in the affirmative or the negative. On the former side we have (1) the probability amounting to moral certainty, that whenever any embodied mind has experienced a change, a certain material change has preceded; (2) the absence of any accepted evidence, except in traditions handed down from more credulous ages, of the existence of particular minds not embodied; and (3) the establishment of a vast and complex, though incomplete, correspondence between particular kinds or qualities of mental processes and particular organic actions or conditions. On the other side, we have the unique disparity of physical and psychical phenomena, and the apparent arbitrariness of the connexion between the two. We do not in the least see *why* movements of nerve particles should produce feelings, and can quite easily conceive the whole series of states which compose our consciousness continuing without these physical antecedents or concomitants; hence it is inferred that the latter cannot be the real causes of the former. The force of this argument, such as it is, is perhaps somewhat strengthened by the occultness of the connexion; we have no means of observing or definitely inferring the kind of motions of matter that immediately precede mental phenomena. I do not refer to important ethical arguments drawn from the need of a future state to realise justice or to establish the required connexion between virtue and happiness, or to the vaguer reasoning based on the desires and expectations of continued existence commonly found among men, since it can hardly be suggested that these have been materially affected by historical biology. But taking the controversy as argued apart from ethical considerations, I cannot perceive that the force either of the argument from the actual closeness and universality of the connexion between psychical and physical fact and the modifying influence exercised by the body on the mind, or of the opposite argument from the arbitrariness, occultness, and conceivable dissolubility of the connexion, will be affected to any extent worth considering by the Darwinian theory or any other theory of evolution. There is, however, a new argument, which I may call the argument from continuity.

If we suppose the process of change thus traced to be perfectly gradual and continuous, another argument emerges when we carry the process back until mind vanishes altogether: it is this argument that I propose to call the Argument from Continuity. It is contended that if the highest, most mental phenomena of organised beings are connected by an unbroken series of infinitesimal differences with the lowest (to whose existence we should commonly not apply the term 'mental' or 'psychical' at all), and even with the phenomena of inorganic matter, there is no point at which the existence of mind, as an independent entity, can be conceived to begin. Probably much of the alarm occasioned among anti-materialists by the theories of Evolution and Natural Selection has been due to the supposed force of this argument. It has been thought that mind could not be independent of matter, if man was gradually developed out of a monkey, and the monkey out of a polyp, and so on. To this argument there are two answers.

Firstly, it is not really strengthened by the theory of evolution of species: its force—whatever that may be—is essentially derived from the undeniable fact that each individual man has been gradually developed out of a portion of organised matter, of which the manner of existence was not more psychical than the polyp's; it cannot, therefore, matter much whether his race has gone through a similar course of change or has not. This difficulty was always, I conceive, presented in full force by the known history of any individual organism, and I do not see that it is materially increased by the completest acceptance of a similar gradual evolution of the human species. The process by which the admittedly soulless organism grows into that supposed to be soul-possessing is indefinitely more rapid in the case of the individual; but I do not see how this difference in rate of change affects the difficulty of conceiving how the connexion of an immortal soul with the gradually changing material organism commences.

Secondly, I am prepared to challenge the validity of the whole argument from continuity against the independent existence of mind. So far as I understand it, it rests on a supposed difficulty in believing that a new thing has come into existence quite gradually. Now I quite admit that it is difficult for us to understand how any really new fact can begin to be at all. But this difficulty has to be overcome, it would seem, by most modern schools of thought in the case of individual minds. For on the one hand they can hardly deny that any particular mind—even if we mean no more by this term than the stream of transient phenomena, thoughts, feelings, and volitions, of which we have direct experience—is a new fact. That is, they cannot deny that it is totally unlike whatever physical facts antecede or accompany it; and they are not commonly prepared to contend that it is composed of pre-existent thoughts, emotions, etc., rearranged in new relations. The 'hylozoism' on which such a contention may be based, has, I think, little place in English philosophical thought. On the other hand, we have equally to admit that this new fact, so far as known, actually begins to be between certain narrow limits of time. If this be granted, I do not see that a perfectly gradual beginning is harder to accept than an abrupt one; on the contrary I should say it was certainly easier. There is no doubt a certain difficulty in imaginatively tracing a thing to its origin, if that has to be reached through an infinite series of indefinitely small changes. But this is only Zeno's old puzzle as to Achilles catching the tortoise, turned round and applied to the beginning instead of the end of a finite quantity of infinitesimally divisible changes, and there is no reason why we should be specially troubled by this ancient paradox in considering the question of the independent existence and possible survival of the soul.

§ 3. I have spoken so far of mind regarded as a whole (or of mental phenomena taken generally). I find, however, that some persons consider it fundamentally important in discussing the relation of Mind and Body to draw a distinction between different kinds of mental fact. They are prepared to admit that the kind of fact, which we distinguish as 'feelings,' or 'sensations,' or 'sense-perceptions'—so far as they guide organic action—may have been completely caused by movements of organic matter; but they maintain that this cannot be the case with other kinds of psychical phenomena. Especially is this maintained with regard to knowledge generally, or certain special kinds or elements of knowledge—such as the immediate knowledge of the unity, permanence, identity of the conscious self, or the axioms of arithmetic or geometry, or perhaps abstract notions generally, etc. Much controversy has been carried on about these distinctions, and many persons still seem concerned to maintain that 'general notions,' 'primitive judgments,' or perhaps the synthetic unity in judgments generally and so forth, cannot be derived from sensations, rather than that sensations cannot be derived from processes of organic matter. Indeed some of those who contend most strongly that *knowledge* cannot properly be regarded as the function of a material organism seem willing to admit that feeling should be so regarded. This view seems to me to emphasise unduly a distinction which, though important, is less important than the distinction which it overlooks. I do not wish to under-estimate the unlikeness that exists between different species of mental phenomena; in particular between cognitions of any kind and the feelings from which it is sought to derive them. But no difference of this kind seems to me at all equal to the disparity that I find between psychical facts as a whole and the physical facts with which physiology leads us to connect them. Therefore if we once admit that the movement of particles of matter is an adequate cause of the most elementary feeling, I see no firm ground on which we can argue that it cannot be an adequate cause of the most refined and complicated thought.

I conclude, then, that the historical method, as applied to Anthropology on the basis of Darwin's theory, leaves the metaphysical problem of the relation of mind and matter exactly where it was. It remains to consider how far our study of the nature of mind, so far as it is an object of empirical knowledge, of 'subjective observation and analysis,' is affected by investigations of its past history, *i.e.* how far Psychology is dominated by Psychogony.

§ 4. Now the investigation of the origin and growth of mental phenomena and faculties has, as is well known, occupied a large share of the attention of

English psychologists since the middle of the last century; and has attained results of undoubted interest, in the ascertainment of the laws of co-existence and sequence of mental phenomena. I think, however, that even the psychological import of these results has often been misconceived. In fact it seems to me that a fundamental mistake of method has been made, favoured by the difficulty and obscurity which attend the introspective observation and analysis of mental phenomena. I have already discussed the subject in the third lecture (*Relation of Philosophy to Psychology*), and will now only just refer to the confusion which seems to me to have taken place between psychical antecedents and psychical elements. We might almost say that through this confusion Psychogony or Historical Psychology had, in some minds, completely taken the place of any other. A study of the history of mind as it has gradually *become* what it is, has illegitimately presented itself as a Sensationalist theory of mind as it is now, all thought being reduced to supposed elements of feeling. And it is noteworthy that by a second illogicality the Sensationalism has led to Materialism. For when the more characteristic states and processes of the fully developed mind have been thus pseudo-chemically decomposed into their supposed elements, then—as all intellectual content has vanished in an imaginary chaos of atomic feelings, the material concomitant of the elementary feeling naturally becomes prominent to the reflective mind that is performing this analysis, and presents itself as the real process.

'*Principiis obsta*'—let us refuse at the outset to be led by false analysis into this confusion of conditions and constituents. Observe I do not depreciate the Associational Psychology in tracing the history of beliefs, the antecedent conditions under which they arise; I am only considering the relation of this to the question of what actually exists in mind here and now. No 'analysis' of any conception or belief can, I conceive, show it to be something other than careful introspection shows it to be. Analysis can only ascertain conditions, antecedents, and concomitants. For example, Space does not mean to me successive feelings of movement, conceived as simultaneous from association with simultaneous feelings of touch, though this may describe the process by which I have come to have the notion of Space. Similarly in Ethics, my own Pleasure is none the more *now* the sole object of my desire and volition even if it were proved—which I do not hold—that it was so originally to my remote ancestors. The apparent bindingness of a rule of duty—Another's greater good to be preferred to my own lesser good, or Similar cases to be treated similarly—is none the less 'intuitive' because the apprehension of it is shown to be not 'innate.'

But, it may be said, granting that the question what our thoughts, emotions, or volitions actually are cannot be affected by any investigation of the process by which they have come to be what they are, still such investigation may have an important bearing on the more interesting because more difficult question, whether they are what they ought to be. The method of introspective observation, it may be said, has commonly professed to do more than give us a mere inventory of our thoughts; it has professed to give us a criterion for determining their validity; and it is this pretension rather than the former that has been successfully traversed and overthrown by historical psychology, or 'psychogony.' And, no doubt, the most interesting part of the controversy between the 'psychogonical' and 'introspective' methods of studying mind has had reference to this question of the validity of beliefs commonly taken as primary and intuitive.

§ 5. Let us consider, then, how far and in what way the validity of such beliefs can be affected by an investigation of their origin and history. At this point, however, it seems to me that we are inevitably drawn from Psychology—or Psychology of the individual as such—into Sociology, or, if you like to call it so, Sociological Psychology. For perhaps the most noteworthy change that has taken place in this study during the last thirty years consists in the increased recognition of the fundamental importance of the 'social factor' in the development of the mind of the individual. It could not, indeed, ever have been denied that a most important part of the conscious thought and feeling of any individual received its character — whether by inherited tendencies or by sympathetic apprehension or both combined — from the current thoughts and prevalent emotions of the society of which he was a member; and that, accordingly, any adequate attempt to trace the development of his conscious life must soon include or pass into a sociological investigation. This, at any rate, is recognised in the work of J. S. Mill, from which, a generation ago, I and many others learnt our 'Logic of the Moral Sciences.' That "what we now are and do" is "the result mainly of the qualities produced in us by the whole previous history of humanity," Mill, after Comte, enforced with as much emphasis as could be desired. He seems, however, to have held that the sociological laws obtained by a study of this history of humanity ought to be shown to be derivative from certain ultimate laws of human nature, independently ascertained : since—to quote his words—" Men, in a state of society, are still men : their actions and passions are obedient to the laws of individual human nature. Men are not, when brought together, converted into another kind of substance, with different properties; as hydrogen and oxygen are different from water, or as hydrogen, oxygen, carbon, and azote are different from nerves, muscles, and tendons. Human beings in society have no properties but those which are derived from, and may be resolved into, the laws of the nature of individual man."[1]

Now it is undeniable that the aggregate of the actions of man in society constitute a more complex fact than the aggregate of the actions of any single individual; society being the whole of which individuals are parts. But it does not follow that, as

[1] *Logic*, bk. vi. ch. vii. § 1.

Mill conceives, a psychology exists or can be constructed independent of sociology, and such that all the laws ascertained by the latter are capable of being resolved into the more elementary laws of the former. In saying that 'men in a state of society are *still* men,' it is implied that we have some means of knowing them adequately *out* of a state of society: just as—to take Mill's analogy—we are able to ascertain adequately the properties of hydrogen and oxygen, apart from their composition in water. But I cannot perceive that we have any such means of knowing the properties of men in this supposed elementary, non-social, condition,—so far, at least, as the most important and interesting departments of their mental life are concerned. The men whom we are able to observe are all social beings who have grown up from infancy under social influences: and, if in studying the mental phenomena of such a being we abstract hypothetically all that is due to sympathy and imitation, and endeavour to ascertain the laws of what remains, the result we obtain will not carry us far towards explaining the thoughts and emotions of actual men. We may perhaps study, without taking the social factor into account, the conditions and laws of sensation, appetite, volition in its most elementary forms, and the revival and association of such phenomena: but if we contemplate any of the processes of thought that involve language, or any of the more refined and complex emotions, and endeavour to ascertain the causes of their actual characteristics, we are inevitably carried from the study of the mere individual into the study of the society of which he is a member, and the whole inquiry into the validity of beliefs must, I conceive, fall into this department of study. The current beliefs, the prevailing sentiments, in a given society at a given time, are no doubt beliefs and sentiments of a certain aggregate of individuals: but we have generally speaking no means of tracing and explaining their development and diffusion in the consciousness of the great mass of individuals who entertain them: for the purposes of our cognition, they must be treated as social facts.

Now there is not, I conceive, at the present day any doubt that the investigation of the laws of change in the prevalent beliefs of human societies is a most important element of the whole study of sociology— or of history, in the ordinary sense. Nor, again, is there any doubt that this study, being a department of history, ought to be pursued according to a historical method.

But much more than this seems to be maintained by the writers who have recently emphasised the claims of the Historical Method especially in the different departments of the theory of practice, in ethics, jurisprudence, politics. They have meant by it not merely an investigation of the sequence in which beliefs have actually succeeded one another as social phenomena, and the causes or laws of this sequence; but also a method for determining—what, after all, is the most interesting question with regard to any class of human beliefs—viz., how far they are true or false. It is as thus regarded that the Historical Method is sometimes said to have invaded and transformed these departments of thought, and it is as thus regarded that it appears to claim the place and undertake the function of that department of Philosophy which I have called Epistemology—the investigation of criteria of the truth or falsehood of current beliefs. I propose to examine its claims to decide questions belonging to this investigation in the next lecture.

LECTURE VIII

RELATION OF PHILOSOPHY TO SOCIOLOGY

§ 1. In the last lecture I have been engaged in examining the relation of Philosophy to History : and especially in criticising closely the pretensions of the Historical Method to have 'invaded and transformed all departments of thought.' So far I have used the term 'History' and 'Historical Method' in the widest possible sense, to include any study of the past pursued with a view to the explanation of the present. It is in this widest sense that the universality of application of the Historical Method seemed to me most plausible. But there is a narrower and more ordinary sense, more in harmony with the current use of the word 'history' unqualified, according to which 'Historical Method' would imply a study not of past facts generally, but of past *social* facts, especially thoughts and sentiments; and it is with this narrower meaning that the current enthusiasm for the Historical Method is perhaps most frequently connected. In this narrower sense we might equally well—or perhaps better—term it the *Sociological* Method.

At this point, therefore, I turn definitely to the discussion of the Relation of Philosophy to Sociology. It is only with one special department of Sociology that we shall be, in the main, concerned. In order to present a general view of the subject-matter of this department I may conveniently begin the discussion by recalling what was said in the last lecture, as to the extent to which Sociology has successfully invaded, during the last generation, the peculiarly English study which I have called Psychogony; the inquiry, that is, into the growth and development of Mind.

I think it important to dwell on this relation of Psychology to Sociology, because the part of psychological study which is specially influenced by the social factor is just that part in which the subject-matter of Psychology and Philosophy most nearly coincide—the region of thought and the more refined and complex emotions. I agree with the late Professor Croom Robertson in holding that the non-recognition of the social factor in Psychology is a grave defect in the method of the older English psychologists. As he says:—"They can hardly be blamed for not anticipating the importance of heredity: but in the last century, as at other times, it was sufficiently plain that children, being born into the world, are born into society, and are under overpowering social influences before (if one may so speak) they have any chance of being their proper selves."[1] Of these influences, on the intellectual side, language

[1] *Philosophical Remains*, 1894, p. 66.

is the great medium. Even to a definite apprehension of particular objects in space children are effectively helped by the fact that there is a current medium of social communication about things, the advantage of which is forced upon them. But this is not the chief point. As all are agreed, it is for purposes of general knowledge that language is most indispensable; and the language spoken by a race of men is an accurate index to the grade of intellectual comprehension, the stage of intellectual progress reached by the community; and to this grade the child is introduced through the speech of others. There is a ready-made scheme of thought given to us *en bloc* with the words of our mother-tongue, which we use our natural subjective experience mainly to decipher and verify. I might go on to show how similarly, though more indefinitely, each one's habitual emotions and volitions are influenced by sympathy with those of the maturer human beings among whom he grows up. But I am not giving a course of lectures on Psychology, and I have said enough to indicate the place of the social factor in it.

The individual adult man, then, as known to us by experience, is what he is in consequence of having grown up in social relations; and we have no ground for saying—as Mill has done in the passage already quoted[1]—that the laws or uniformities of his actual behaviour as a member of a community are derived from the laws of his *hypothetical* behaviour as an abstract individual.

[1] Cf. p. 153 above.

It is not more true that Sociology is derived from and presupposes Psychology, than that Psychology, except of a very limited kind, presupposes Sociology; because of the fundamental importance in considering the phenomena of the individual mind of the effects of sympathy, and of the communication of ideas and feelings from mind to mind. Even the most original individual is to a great extent the child or creature of his age; he shares the common thought, the common sentiment of his society at a given time.[1]

On this point, there is, I conceive, but little difference of opinion among different schools of thought at the present day. It would be generally agreed that in seeking a historical explanation of the whole complex succession of thoughts, sentiments, and habits that forms the intellectual life of an educated human being in a civilised society we are inevitably led from Psychology or Psychogony into Sociology or Social Science. We have to study the development of the social mind which the individual shares.

We have then, henceforward, to concentrate attention on this department of Sociological inquiry: the study of the common sentiments and thoughts, opinions and conceptions, the fundamental assumptions which tend to be shared by the members of a society,[2] or at least by the educated and thoughtful members,

---

[1] I may observe that in some places Mill's language seems to acknowledge this to the utmost (cf. *Logic*, bk. vi. ch. x.); in others, as the one before quoted, he seems entirely to overlook it. This is due to a combination of two streams of speculation—the Comtian Sociology, and the English Psychology of his father, James Mill—which he has imperfectly harmonised.

[2] Often a society far more extensive than any one state.

at any given time; but which change from age to age, so that a man born in one age tends to acquire a different set from a man born in another. Of this common thought any individual, even a highly educated individual, usually possesses only a very small part, in the fulness with which it belongs to his society as a whole; but it is characteristic of a really educated man that he has always in some degree, though in an indefinitely varying degree, a general acquaintance with the rest and a vague sympathetic apprehension of it. For example, those of us who know least of science have some general apprehension of the dominant conceptions of current Physics—conservation of mass and energy; and of current Biology—evolution, natural selection, and the struggle for existence. Those of us who know least of Logic know that the present tendencies of thought are inductive and experimental. Those of us who know least of History know that we are living in an age in which the Historical Method is antiquating the old unhistorical dogmatism in Politics and cognate studies. Those of us who know least of Philosophy, and would have considerable difficulty in constructing a cogent argument for the belief in the Uniformity of Nature, are aware that it is a mark of enlightenment to assume that 'miracles do not happen.'

Now there is not, I think, any doubt that the investigation of the important changes that have historically occurred in the prevalent beliefs of human societies is an important study: and the students of Sociology have, I conceive, a right to claim it for their own, and to demand that it be pursued as a branch of a comprehensive inquiry into the evolution of human society as a whole. Especially in the departments of Ethics and Politics, with which I have been specially concerned, do I recognise the importance of studying in historical order the variations in political ideas and beliefs in their double relation partly as cause and partly as effect of change in political facts; and similarly in studying the changes in ethical ideas in connexion with changes in other elements of social structure and in the relations between societies. And of course in both these studies, since they are departments of history, we must use a historical method.

§ 2. But what we have now to consider is not the general interest of this inquiry as a branch of Sociology: but its importance in relation to the question of the validity of the thoughts and beliefs investigated. The question is how far a sociological inquiry into the history of our beliefs can and ought to affect our philosophical view of their truth or falsehood. To simplify the consideration of this question let us consider first the *destructive*, and then the *constructive* effect of such an inquiry, *i.e.* let us first ask how far the historical study of beliefs leads us to regard them as untrustworthy, and then how far it tends to prove them trustworthy and valid.

Here I may first note that a mere investigation of the facts—the actual diversity and succession of human beliefs in such subjects as ethics and politics and theology—without any establishment of *laws* of change, does seem to tend to be connected with a general scepticism as to the validity of the doctrines studied; though the exact nature of the connexion is difficult to determine. The scepticism is, I think, partly the effect and partly the cause of the concentration of the student's mind on his historical research. It partly tends to result from historical study, because of the vast and bewildering variety of conflicting beliefs, all strongly, even unhesitatingly entertained at certain times and places, which this study marshals before us. The student's own most fundamental and most cherished convictions seem forced, as it were, to step down from their secure pedestals, and to take their places in the endless line that is marching past. Other conflicting convictions, for which their holders have been ready to die, have gone before and are out of sight: others as short-lived are coming after, which the transient generations ahead will probably embrace with equal tenacity. Thus to the historian, who is an animal of larger discourse than the plain man, looking before and after in a fuller sense, the whole defiling train of beliefs tends to become something from which he sits apart,

> Beholding besides thoughts the end of thought,
> Hearing oblivion beyond memory.

Every portion of this series seems to have lost power to hold his own reason in the grip of true conviction: for peace's sake, he accepts the beliefs that are pressed on him by public opinion in his own age and country; but in his heart he believes in nothing but history. I think that some effect of this kind is actually produced, in varying intensity, on the minds of many students of the history of opinion: but I cannot regard it as normal and legitimate—indeed I doubt whether even those who feel this sceptical effect most strongly would usually maintain their scepticism as a conclusion attained by any explicit rational procedure, admitting of logical tests.

So far as Ethics is concerned, I have elsewhere contended[1] that the ascertainment of the origin and development of beliefs cannot logically have any such *general* effect in destroying our confidence in beliefs actually held, as has been sometimes confusedly supposed by those who have considered it important to show that a system of moral intuitions—or at least the faculty of moral intuition—was *innate* and not derived or developed. To show that any such intuition was caused in a particular way can have no tendency to make a reasonable man regard it as invalid unless it can be also shown that the causes operating were such as would tend to make it untrue; since it is a fundamental assumption of sociological, as of all other scientific inquiries, that *every* belief must have been caused in some particular way,—sociological beliefs no less than ethical. But in order to *prove* that any belief—say any ethical belief—is the result of causes tending to produce an erroneous belief, we must know that some other ethical belief is true, for error is only proved by proving inconsistency with truth. *General* disbelief therefore

---

[1] See *Methods of Ethics*, bk. iii. ch. i. § 4.

cannot be logically justified in this way either in ethics or in any other department: though doubtless *primâ facie* general *scepticism* may be explained, by the complex divergence and conflict of beliefs which this historical inquiry shows us. And certainly I should rather regard this sceptical effect of the historical method as a kind of disorder, if I may so say, which is liable to attack weakly organised systems of belief, while it is powerless against those more strongly organised—those, I mean, as to which there is a consensus of experts now established. I pointed out before[1] that historical study has now no similar effects in mathematics or physical science or astronomy: the student of the history of these sciences traces the bizarre opinions and fantastic methods of earlier *savants* without feeling or causing the slightest distrust of our own methods or conclusions. To take a historic example: when we learn the great Kepler's view of the celestial harmonies produced by the various and varying velocities of the several planets and of the gratification these harmonies gave to the sentient soul inhabiting the sun, we are entertained and perhaps instructed; but it never occurs to us to question that we are right in neglecting this peculiar line of speculation. But no doubt, in departments where fundamental controversy and divergence of method exist among ourselves,—as they do in Ethics—the scepticism which such present controversies and divergencies tend to generate draws further nutriment from historical study,

[1] [Lecture VI. § 2, pp. 127 ff.]

owing to the ampler range and greater complexity of variation which the history of doctrine brings before us.

This is a natural and perhaps inevitable result of contemplating man historically. But to yield to it seems to me mere weakness; and it not unfrequently leads to a curious, contradictory state of mind in the historian who does yield to it. He finds his fundamental beliefs in ethics, politics, theology, philosophy, as I have said, drop from him, in spite of the apparent self-evidence with which they present themselves—or once presented themselves—to him, and, as he knows, to others also: but to his historic beliefs—and even his prehistoric conjectures as to (*e. g.*) the structure of polity in primitive Greece, the conditions of property in primitive Rome, the marriage relations of our Aryan ancestors—he clings with a passionate intensity of conviction which is in singular contrast to the slenderness of the evidence that it is possible to adduce in their support.

No doubt, as I before hinted, the historical study of beliefs in such departments as ethics, politics, or theology is sometimes the effect as much as the cause of this kind of scepticism: the mind, wearied of the vain effort to ascertain what is true, settles down more and more to the task of ascertaining what has been held; here, at least, the student feels, some steady progress and stable results may be hoped for. This is human and natural enough: but it is human surely in a bad sense — human weakness. Conflict and controversy on fundamental points, with adequately trained, subtle, and penetrating intellects, afford adequate grounds for self-distrust, for circumspection, for re-examination of our fundamental assumptions and methods, for continued patient efforts to enter into the point of view of opponents; but they are surely not adequate grounds for the abandonment of the highest interests of reason and humanity.

§ 3. So much for the general scepticism in ethics and politics that is liable to result from historical study. But the question remains how far an examination of the particular process by which particular moral or political beliefs have grown up may prove that the beliefs in question are false or misleading owing to certain definite tendencies to cause error which we find in the process.

Now no doubt if, when we trace the history of any belief, we find demonstrably false opinions among its antecedents, this discovery suggests that the belief in question is also false. But though it *suggests* this, it by no means proves it. So far, indeed, as the belief in question is held not as self-evident, but as an inference from antecedent premises, the demonstration of the falsity of the premises certainly removes the ground for believing. Thus I think no study of historical morality can leave unimpaired the influence of mere custom and opinion on the reflective individual, or of the blind emotional impulse normally connected with custom and tradition. That anything is right, *because* an overwhelming majority of human beings think so and act accordingly, becomes a manifestly untenable inference, when we contemplate the monstrous beliefs as to right and wrong which this overwhelming majority has entertained and acted on in previous ages.

But the case is quite different when the antecedent false opinions are merely found to have been among the causes of the belief in question, and are not put forward as reasons for holding it. It may be that it is the destiny of the human intellect to progress through error to truth; and the history of established sciences, solidly supported at the present time on the agreement of experts using substantially the same method, shows that this has in fact not rarely been the case. Whether we can, as Comte thought, find the fundamental law of the evolution of truth from error in a 'law of three stages'—theological, metaphysical, positive—is a disputed question which I reserve for a subsequent lecture : but the more general, vaguer proposition that truth grows gradually out of error, and, so far as we can see, would not have been reached except by the way of error, this will hardly be disputed. Hence, however clear may be the historical connexion between some moral rule which we are disposed to regard as binding and some primitive custom which we unhesitatingly condemn as pernicious or some belief which we unhesitatingly reject as absurd, the later belief may still be true though that which preceded and partly caused it was false.

Let us take one or two instances : Punishment, we all agree, ought to be inflicted on criminals : and it is still a widely-spread belief — I have seen it maintained by competent writers in journals of repute

—that such infliction is desirable in itself, and not merely in view of its consequences in preventing future crime in the way of determent, reformation, or disablement, as utilitarians hold. This, indeed, is one of the most important points at issue between utilitarians and their opponents. Well, there is no doubt, when we view punishment as a political and social fact and trace its history, that the historical link of filiation between the sentiment that impels to punishment and the earlier sentiment that impels to revenge is unmistakable. The blood-feud is, in earlier stages of society, the customary and only effective means of repressing manslaughter; and as the consequence of this—or rather perhaps as a concomitant effect of the causes to which this is due—there grows up a specially intense sense of the duty of revenge. Well, as the process of civilisation goes on, Government puts down the blood-feud, being moved to do so, no doubt, largely by the weakening and disturbing effect of private war of all kinds. Then Christianity comes, preaching the duty of forgiveness. And ultimately our present complex state of feeling is generated, that the individual wronged ought to forgive; this is his sacred duty; but that society or the Government, which 'beareth not the sword in vain,' ought to punish. Now I think this history certainly suggests the truth of the utilitarian view of punishment rather than the older intuitional view. But though it suggests it, it certainly does not disprove the latter: it still remains quite possible to regard the old blood-feud as 'rude justice' and the sentiment connected with it as having a good and bad element —justice and revenge blended. Then, it may be said, under the influence of civilisation the right and proper moral feeling that manslaughter ought to be punished is distinguished and separated from the wrong personal feeling that *I* ought to avenge the manslaughter of a kinsman. To use a phrase of Mr. Spencer's, it may be said that 'Revenge' is a 'pro-ethical' sentiment which preceded the true ethical sentiment of justice. Well, I cannot deny that this is an admissible view of the process that sociology brings clearly before us: and therefore any inference from the sociological *aperçu* to the decision of the ethical issue is not logically conclusive.

Let us turn to another sentiment, which I select as one that cannot be said to be now prevalent,—the sentiment against the re-marriage of widows. I select it because, though there is no general condemnation of this act, Auguste Comte, the founder of Sociology, in laying down rules for his Positivist Community, carried the idea of monogamy to this point of severity for men as well as women. I mention this, as otherwise the sentiment might be thought to be necessarily connected with Christian ideas of resurrection and a future life. Well, it would not, I think, be difficult to show the historic connexion of this sentiment with the barbaric impulse not only to make offerings of food on the grave of a deceased chief or brave, but to sacrifice his favourite horse there, and deposit his spear or sword, etc. We see the connecting link in the burning of the Hindoo widow on the funeral pile:

which our Government in India has thought it right to put down by law, against (I believe) the strong moral sentiment of the Hindoos. The connexion seems unmistakable, but here again no logical inference is possible against the validity of the later sentiment. It may be said that the barbarous belief that the departed chief required food and spear was a mere husk of the true intuition that his soul was immortal: and that the sentiment of the Hindoo widow is noble, though its expression is cruel and exaggerated.

To sum up: I think that the sceptical or destructive effect often attributed to, and sometimes really exercised by, the study of the history of opinion does not really rest on a logical basis. In my next lecture I shall consider how far this study can have a positive effect, in the way of enabling us to find truth among the diversities of opinion studied.

LECTURE IX

RELATION OF PHILOSOPHY TO SOCIOLOGY (*continued*)

§ 1. In the last lecture I examined the bearing of the inquiry into the development of human knowledge and beliefs—knowledge being belief taken as well-grounded—on the philosophical question of the validity of the beliefs, and especially of such beliefs as do not present themselves either as exactly self-evident or as conclusions demonstrated from self-evident premises, though in ordinary thought they appear to be assumed unquestioningly.[1] Such beliefs, as a part of a generally accepted system, have at any rate, no less than those that present themselves as strictly self-evident or demonstrated, the characteristics of general acceptance. I have accordingly called them, in Ethics, the beliefs of Common Sense: and this term is convenient to suggest the sociological as well as the philosophical point of view from which such beliefs may be regarded.

I began by pointing out that, owing to the overwhelming importance of the social factor in the

[1] Cf. the belief in the existence of the external world or that in Universal Causation.

causation of the beliefs of a normal human individual, the methods of Psychology and Sociology blend in this inquiry, and the method of Sociology dominates.

Our fundamental question, then, was: How do the results of sociological study of beliefs, and especially of the fundamental beliefs commonly accepted, affect the philosophical consideration of them?

In examining this question I thought it well to divide it into two parts, and consider separately, first the *destructive* and *negative* effect of sociological or historical study of the beliefs of Common Sense—its effect in the way of producing scepticism, general or particular; and then its positive or constructive effect, in the way of supporting or confirming the validity of such beliefs.

As regards the first part of the question, I tried to show that the vague general scepticism which the study of the history of opinion is liable to produce, is only effective in a department of thought which is still in a condition of fundamental controversy, and only effective in a secondary way as adding strength to the doubts which this controversy itself reasonably produces. For, in departments like physical science, in which 'consensus of experts' has been attained, historical study has, as I showed, no such force: a study of the history of alchemy does not shake our confidence in modern chemistry, nor a study of astrology our confidence in astronomy.

The question still remains whether an examination of the particular antecedent history of particular current beliefs may not prove their falsity. And, as

I said, if, when we trace the history of any belief, we find demonstrably false opinions among its antecedents, the discovery certainly *suggests* that the belief in question is false. But it only *proves* this when the belief is held as an inference from premises ascertained to be false: the case is quite different when the false opinions found among the antecedents of the belief in question are not put forward as reasons for holding it. The history of the established sciences shows us truth continually and gradually attained through a strange and bewildering course of mazy and conflicting errors: and we have every reason to regard the antecedence of error as an indispensable condition of the attainment of truth.

§ 2. So much for the sceptical effect of the historical study of human thought. I do not, however, regard this as its main or normal effect: were it so, the prevalent enthusiasm for the Historical Method would be quite unaccountable. This is rather due to the hope or conviction that the proper study of history, and that alone, has the gift of healing the scepticism which the history of beliefs, if crudely and superficially apprehended, no doubt tends to aggravate: that it will yield the patient and duly trained inquirer a clue through the maze of opinions, a criterion by which he may find truth at the last.

Now I am far from wishing to discourage such hopes—so long as they remain merely hopes: but they seem to me in many minds to have transformed themselves into convictions too confident and unhesitating for the present state of our knowledge. I quite admit that a study of the development of human opinion in any department may give us valuable confirmation for conclusions otherwise arrived at as to the right procedure for attaining truth in that department: but I do not see how such conclusions can possibly be established in the first instance by a purely historical method. To show this, let us suppose realised the utmost hopes of the most sanguine student of the science of history: let us suppose that we have ascertained completely the law of development of ethical, political, theological, or philosophical opinion, so that we can state accurately the views which will be generally accepted by the coming generation. We cannot therefore take the foreseen current opinion to be true, any more than the opinion now current: and it would be peculiarly hard for the historical student to do this, as he would do so under the condition of having to hold at the same time that the dissimilar opinions prevalent in previous ages were untrue so far as dissimilar.

Let us take as illustration a political belief. Suppose I foresee, what perhaps was more probable a generation ago than now, that the coming democracy will hold as a universal belief that the will of the numerical majority ought always to be obeyed, and that to resist it is criminal rebellion against rational political order—just as two hundred years ago the corresponding belief was held with regard to resistance to the will of a hereditary monarch. Suppose I foresee certainly that this belief will come, I cannot *therefore* conclude that it will be a true belief. I am not even led any way towards this conclusion: illusions as to the divine right of majorities may come and pass, like illusions as to the divine right of kings: if its validity is to be proved it must be by some other method.

Or, again, take an ethical belief. As I noticed last time, there is a stage in the development of society at which the duty of requiting evil appears to be as intensely felt to be imperative, by the common moral sentiment of the society, as the duty of requiting good. But civilisation gradually makes men regard the blood-feud and the sacred duty of shedding blood for blood, destroying tooth for tooth, as barbaric. Suppose then that I can foresee that the duty of gratitude will hereafter go the way of the duty of resentment, so that the only result of a man's having rendered me gratuitous services will be that I shall regard him with approval as the organ of society for rendering me such services in future, and complain if he leaves off rendering them; leaving it to society to allot him any remuneration for his services that may be expedient.[1] Well, the mere fact that I can foresee that it will come has no tendency to make me judge it good that it should come: or judge that this view of duty will be truer than my own now. I am disposed to go further, and say that unless we start with a thoroughly sceptical or eccentric view as to the attainment of truth in any subject—ethics, politics, theology, or philosophy—unless we bring this to the

---

[1] I take this case, because I seem to discern rudiments of this change actually going on.

study of history or somehow, not logically, derive it from the study, there will be a fundamental difficulty in forecasting the development of opinions, whatever insight into the law of development we may appear to derive from a study of the past. For we shall have some view of our own—say some theory of political or ethical end or method widely accepted here and now—which we shall regard as true: at the same time, as historians, we shall contemplate a long line of divergent opinions in past ages—such as the theological fancy of the divine right of kings, just mentioned, or the metaphysical fiction of the natural rights of man. Surely the unique quality of being *true* which we attribute to the opinions of our own time must make inevitably a very profound difference between the past that leads up to our own truth and the future that takes it as point of departure: so that the line of development in the past can hardly give us much insight into the line of progress in the future. For the present must on this assumption be conceived as a culmination or turning-point in the process of change: the past is seen as a process through error to truth, and the future—so far as change is conceived to go on in fundamental beliefs—must be conceived as the reverse process from truth to error: and it is hard to see how the laws of change and development ascertained by studying the former process can enable us to forecast the latter,—unless history is held to show us examples of similar double processes before, of movements from error to truth, followed by movements from truth to error. Now something may no doubt be said for this view of the history of thought and human society, as resembling the oscillatory movement of a pendulum: but it is hardly a view that the facts, adequately examined, on the whole support; and it is certainly not maintained by any sociologist whose work I know.

§ 3. The lines of answer pursued by Sociologists, in face of the difficulty I have described, are of quite a different kind. In the main, I think we may distinguish two such lines: one of which may perhaps be described as the more philosophical—as being only attractive to minds with some tincture of philosophy—and the other the more popular. But both have the support of philosophers: and it is, as we shall see, possible to combine the two. The formula of the first line of reply is, briefly, that 'knowledge is relative,' of the second that 'knowledge—and human society generally—is progressive.' But a little further explanation of the two formulæ seems desirable, before we pass to consider the lines of answer in detail.

The first line of thought admits to a certain extent the sceptical effect of the historical study of beliefs. It admits, that is, that the process of change in the fundamental beliefs—ethical, political, theological, or philosophical—that we find in examining the process of human thought through the ages does lead us to the conclusion that 'absolute truth' is beyond the attainment of the human mind: but it endeavours to console the student by limiting this admission to 'absolute truth.' It endeavours to reassure him by affirming that though absolute truth is unattainable, relative truth is attainable, and is, in fact, always or necessarily attained: for we may regard the divergent beliefs of different ages and countries as all or for the most part true 'relatively,' and 'relative truth' is all that the mature human mind, taught wisdom by the repeated failure of attempts to penetrate to 'absolute truth,' ought to seek to attain.

Now this answer seems to give great satisfaction to many minds, and therefore I desire to examine it fully. We have already had occasion to refer to it, in dealing with the task of defining Metaphysics. For we found it to be a prevalent view of Metaphysics that it is concerned with 'absolute reality' as contrasted with Science and with Philosophy (so far as merely systematising the Sciences), which are held to be concerned with the 'relative' or 'phenomenal.' At first sight, then, it seems that if Sociology leads to the conclusion that the fundamental beliefs of different ages and countries, speaking broadly, are all 'relatively' though not 'absolutely' true, it leads to a conclusion in harmony with the scientific conception of knowledge: and I think it is partly due to this apparent harmony that this view of the 'relative truth' of successive phases of belief, in the departments of ethics, politics, and to some extent of theology, has come to be so widely accepted.

And, as I before noticed, this view affords a possible —I will not say 'reconciliation,' but *modus vivendi*— between Sociology and Metaphysical Philosophy which is attractive to some minds. For the Sociologist may say that his study of human beliefs does not in any way conflict with, or invade the province of, metaphysical inquiry: it not only leaves room for metaphysics, but even concedes the first rank to it, as the more dignified and profound inquiry. We may take the concession to be sometimes sincere: and so taking it, may consider whether this *modus vivendi* is acceptable.

I propose, then, presently, to examine this answer closely. But before proceeding to this, I should like to point out that it does not entirely help us out of the difficulty in the way of sociological foresight which I have pointed out, it only alters the nature of the difficulty. For though the doctrines of the Relativity of knowledge may enable us to view the divergent beliefs represented in a series from past, through present, to future as all 'relatively true' in spite of their differences, still there is one fundamental truth which will not have this relativity: viz. the truth that all truth is relative. This the Relativist must, I think, admit to be absolutely known, unless his Relativism is to lapse into mere and palpable scepticism: and he will probably hold also that this absolute and fundamental truth ought to be accepted by all enlightened persons. But then the general acceptance by enlightened persons of this fundamental proposition must, it would seem, establish a fundamentally important distinction between the thought of the present age and the thought of the previous ages: for in previous ages the persons engaged in the pursuit of knowledge—the intellectual *élite* of civilised society—pursued truth eagerly, and partially believed themselves to have attained it, without—for the most part—a consciousness of its relativity, or at any rate without a full consciousness. We, on the other hand, or the coming men, are, according to the doctrine I am examining, supposed to have attained this full consciousness. On this point then no further change seems possible, unless we suppose future humanity to lapse from knowledge into ignorance on this point— which would get us into the difficulty before mentioned of conceiving the present as a culmination or turning-point between the two movements, one from error to truth and the other from truth to error. But if no further change is possible, then surely, though in a different way, there must be a profound difference between the past history of belief, in which we trace the succession of generations pursuing absolute truth and mostly holding opinions—ethical, political, theological—conceived to be absolutely true, and the forecast of its future history, in which the pursuit and the consciousness of attainment can only be of relative truth. In view of this profound difference, it would seem that any forecast of the future must be presumptuous; the development of past thought can hardly afford any guidance as to the development of future thought under this essentially different fundamental condition.

For my own part, if I conceive the intellectual *élite* of civilised society, the thoroughly instructed persons, accepting in any department of thought this philosophical 'relativism' pure and simple, with the full impartiality and neutrality as between the divergent beliefs of different ages which appears to constitute its philosophical attraction—I can hardly imagine the pursuit of truth going on at all in that department among these thoroughly instructed persons. The aim of attaining the true ethical or political ideal, the true view of duty and right and ultimate good, either in private conduct or the constitution of society, appears to me worthy of the sustained ardour and devotion which it has in the past actually aroused in philosophical minds: but I cannot imagine how any one should

> Scorn delights and live laborious days

in order to pass from the relative truth of the nineteenth century to the relative truth of the twentieth, supposing the latter to be not a jot more true or less merely relative than the former.

§4. Let us now examine more closely the propositions that 'all our knowledge is relative' or that 'the truth attainable by man is only relative truth.' It might conceivably be interpreted in as many different senses as there are different kinds of relations: but I shall only take note of senses in which the word 'relative' appears to have been actually used in this connexion. First, I would distinguish the meaning or group of meanings of 'relative' that seems most natural from a sociological point of view, from the meaning or group of meanings which is most obvious and usual from a philosophical point of view. From a sociological point of view, the relation implied in affirming 'relativity' of knowledge or truth would be a relation to the structure or functioning of the social organism to which we conceive the beliefs in question to belong, or a relation to the end of social self-preservation to which all the organic functions of the organism are, as we have seen, normally adapted. From a philosophical point of view, on the other hand, when 'relativity' is affirmed of any piece of apparent knowledge, there are two obvious alternative relations which may be implied, *primâ facie* different from the meaning just mentioned, viz. (1) relation of an object known to the knowing mind, and (2) relation to some other object of knowledge. The latter relation is very important in studying the theory of knowledge, but it does not concern us here; for in the present discussion we are assuming a distinction between relative truth and absolute truth, or relative knowledge and knowledge of absolute reality; and, so far as I know or can conceive, the condition of knowing whatever particular thing or truth I may know in relation to some other thing or truth—the other thing being possibly, in the case of a whole, a part of itself —this condition must apply to knowledge of absolute truth or the most real reality, no less than to knowledge of the relative. Whether Space really exists or is merely a form of sense-perception, I must cognise any particular portion of matter which I perceive as in relation to other things in space : whether Time is real or not, I must conceive any change as in relation to antecedent and subsequent changes in time: whether my general conceptions represent absolute realities or merely phenomena, I must conceive the individuals included under any such resemblance as related in the way of resemblance. Even if the real was found on analysis to consist entirely of such relations—as is held by one school of metaphysicians—still the 'relativity' in this sense that was found to be the essence of absolute reality would not be the kind of relativity into which we are now inquiring: for the essential inter-relatedness of reality does not enable us to conceive how the different views of truth held at successive stages of development should all be equally true. For the present, therefore, I confine myself, from the philosophical point of view, to the consideration of 'relativity' in the sense in which it implies some relation of the object known to the knowing mind: and I think it will be convenient to examine first this philosophical sense of 'relativity' and then to proceed to discuss the sociological sense before distinguished.

Now I do not say that no useful meaning can be given to the propositions that 'all our knowledge is relative' to the knowing mind or subject, and that the truth attainable by us is in this sense only relative truth. But so far as I understand the sense in which these propositions are ordinarily enunciated, I certainly think that they contain considerably more error or confusion of thought than truth. If, indeed, it is merely meant that we can only know what is related to our faculty of knowledge, the proposition is at once incontrovertible and insignificant. It is obvious that we can only know what is knowable, and no one ever supposed that we could know what is unknowable. But if the proposition means that we cannot know things as they are in themselves, then—though experience does not justify me in giving it a complete denial—we may fairly say that the proposition expresses the limits of our knowledge and not its essential nature. Briefly I should say that in this sense our knowledge is relative only so far as it is not completely knowledge, does not completely realise our general idea of true knowledge. It is essential to this idea that what we know really is as we know it: but the long process of human error which it is the painful experience of the student of history to survey prevents our affirming with perfect confidence that any portion even of what we now take for scientific knowledge completely realises this idea. But, I maintain, so far as we are right in regarding it as knowledge, real, though not complete, we are right in assuming that the object known really is as we apparently know it; though it may, of course, have other qualities and characteristics which we do not know. If therefore we are to use the term 'relative knowledge or truth' with a meaning at once precise and useful (from a philosophical as distinct from a sociological point of view) I think it can only mean 'the best approximation to knowledge or truth' attainable by the mind to which the knowledge is affirmed to be relative.

I shall have occasion to illustrate this in considering the more properly sociological view of 'relativity of knowledge.' What from this point of view is the relation implied? The meaning that it seems to me natural for the sociologist to take, who is contemplating belief as a social fact, is that the relation is relation to the end of social preservation :—this being the great end to which the whole gradual complex differentiation of social structure as well as the whole combination and mutual dependence of social functions are held to be normally conducive. Or again, 'relative' may mean conducive not to preservation alone but to development or well-being. The difference of the three notions, Preservation, Development, Welfare, is important, and I shall return to it hereafter: but at present I would take the conception of what I may call the sociological end as vaguely representing the three. It is relativity to this end conceived in one or other form that seems to be often meant by the assertion that certain political beliefs were relatively true at the times they were prevalent: the belief in the Divine right of kings at one stage of political development, or at another the belief in an original contract constituting the society and determining the mutual rights of governor and governed. What seems to be meant is that it was expedient for the preservation or development or well-being of the society that these should be currently held. But if this is all that 'relative truth' means, then though the word 'relative' is appropriate enough, the word 'truth' is singularly inappropriate. For we are familiar in ordinary life with beliefs which it is or seems expedient for the society or the individual, under certain conditions, to hold, but which we should never think of calling true, because we know them not to correspond to the facts. If, in order to keep a child from eating plums off a tree in the garden to the detriment of its health, I tell it that there is a wolf lying hidden that will probably pounce upon it if it touches the plums, I endeavour to impart a belief that I feel it to be expedient for the individual child to hold: but I do not therefore call it 'true'—not even 'relatively true.' I know there is no wolf there, so that expediency and truth fall completely apart.

It may be answered 'Yes, they fall apart for you, but not perhaps for the child: the child can only effectively hold the belief that it ought not to eat the plums *in the form* of a belief that a wolf's pounce or something else disagreeable that it can definitely imagine may befall it if it eats them.' Now here we must distinguish the general notion of something disagreeable, and the particular image of a wolf pouncing. Those who are familiar with ethical controversy know that it is a view held by many that the only real meaning of the assertion 'I ought not to do so and so' is that something disagreeable will happen to me if I do. This is not my view: I do not hold that the moral judgment has *only* this egoistic significance: I have argued strongly against this view, and for the essential disinterestedness of our common judgments of right and wrong. But there certainly seem to be not a few persons whose minds cannot find a place for this conception of a disinterested 'ought.' Let us suppose that theirs is the true view: that when the proposition 'I ought to do this' is true it is always also true that 'some harm will happen to me if I do not do it,' and that this second proposition gives the real meaning of the first. Let us grant, what experience certainly indicates, that the 'harm' in some cases is only moral harm, interference with moral growth; but we may still suppose that it is necessarily conceived as physical harm—pain of some kind—by children generally, or by societies in an early stage. Let us suppose this: then we may say, returning to our plums and wolf, that the general idea we wish to convey to the child—that something disagreeable will happen to it—is relatively true: it is ethical truth in the only form in which the child's mind *can* take it in: but that the image of the wolf is altogether fictitious, though it may be an expedient fiction as the easiest or only means effective to induce the child to accept the relative truth.

I have tried to make this distinction clear, because I admit the 'relativity of truth' in ethics and politics up to a certain point, and therefore it becomes important to distinguish in current beliefs the element of relative truth from the element of expedient fiction. We may apply it to the fundamental political beliefs of the earlier period of modern European history—the period leading up to the French Revolution—the belief in the natural rights of man and the social contract as a means of preserving them. We may regard it as a relative truth that a man had a natural right to Freedom, as being the only form in which the proposition that a man ought to have freedom in a well-ordered society could be then strongly held: but the belief that our ancestors had actually had this freedom in a state of nature, and had formally resigned it by entering into a social compact, is not properly regarded as a relative truth, but only as a fiction, an erroneous belief possibly convenient as a means for conveying the relative truth into minds on which the relative truth alone would not take sufficiently strong hold without the fiction.

This being granted, we have now to observe that a reasoned judgment as to the relative truth or the partial fictitiousness of a current belief requires us to suppose ourselves in possession of absolute ethical truth —or at any rate to suppose our own belief so much nearer the truth than the current belief we are examining that we take it as an absolute standard for judging the current belief. For to know that any belief is fictitious, *i.e.* not correspondent to fact, we must suppose ourselves to know what the fact is. Again, to know that any ethical or political belief is expedient though false, we must know that it is the best available means to the attainment of the right end: we must know therefore what the right end is, wherein social well-being, etc., consists, and be able to judge of the conduciveness of means to the end. The latter we may learn from Sociology, as Sociology progresses; but what the end is at which we ought to aim we cannot learn from Sociology. Any judgment we make as to the rightness of a practical end—that it is an end we ought to aim at—must be a fundamental ethical judgment; which we cannot regard as in its turn a merely relative truth.

LECTURE X

RELATION OF PHILOSOPHY TO SOCIOLOGY (*continued*)

§ 1. We have noted that though the ascertainment of the antecedents of a belief cannot furnish a cogent demonstration of its falsity—not even when we find false beliefs among these antecedents—still the mere contemplation of the diversity and change in beliefs which human history exhibits in such subjects as Ethics, Politics, and Theology, which are still in a condition of fundamental controversy, has a tendency to produce an attitude of general scepticism with regard to them. The question then is whether Sociology, attaining a knowledge of laws of change and development in this department of social fact, can cure the scepticism which history alone, presenting us with a mere spectacle of diversity and conflict, tends to produce. There appear to be two chief ways of meeting this scepticism, which I distinguished as *Relativism* and *Progressivism*.

The former, while resigning the hope of attaining 'absolute truth,' affirms that the diverse beliefs of different ages are all 'relatively true.' In interpreting the ambiguous term 'relative' I distinguished the meaning that properly belongs to the philosophical point of view—where 'relative' is contrasted with 'absolute' knowledge—from that which properly belongs to the sociological point of view. From the philosophical point of view, I took 'relative' to mean 'in relation to the knowing mind.' I pointed out that if it be merely meant that the fundamental beliefs of past ages were, and the divergent beliefs of other contemporary Societies are, normal to the human mind in a certain stage of its development, and ours can be no more, then this notion of relative hides a purely sceptical view. The 'relatively true' beliefs are none the less contradictory for being in a sense normal; and if we once conceive our own fundamental beliefs to be beliefs which a future generation will discard as erroneous, exactly as we have discarded those of the past, then I do not see how, while regarding them thus, they can maintain anything like the same hold over our minds as they would if we regarded them as absolutely true.[1] The only point of knowledge, free from scepticism, is just this relativity, and we cannot really conceive any further progress as regards this fundamental distinction of relative and absolute.

If again the term 'relatively true' is interpreted so as to avoid this scepticism, it must mean either that the past belief so described was the nearest approximation to the truth which the human mind in this particular stage of its development could reach, or

[1] The word 'true' has no magic to neutralise the scepticism latent in the word 'relative.'

that such belief was expedient, though wholly or partially false.

The latter brings us to the meaning of 'relative' which is most appropriate from the sociological point of view: *i.e.* implying relation as a means to an end of social preservation or welfare. But to know that an ethical or political belief, prevalent in a past age, was expedient though wholly or partially false, we must know that it was a means to the attainment of the end—whether defined as social preservation, social welfare, or otherwise—by conduciveness to which expediency is properly estimated: and similarly, in order to judge on adequate grounds that a belief is partially or approximately true, we must ourselves be in possession, if not of absolute truth on the subject, at any rate of something which we have reason to regard as a nearer approximation. In either case we assume ourselves to be in a fundamentally superior position, in respect of truth and knowledge, to that of the past age which we are judging. But, on the one hand, it is difficult to see how a purely sociological study of belief as a social fact with no other criterion of truth than sociology affords can justify us in making this assumption; while, on the other hand, if we do make it, we thereby introduce so fundamental a difference between the present age and all past ages that it is difficult to see how a study of the changes of belief in the past can enable us to predict the future course of its development.

§ 2. Here, however, it may be said that this impartial relativism pure and simple, which I have described, though it may be entertained by some students of the history of thought who have had no training in modern science nor attained a grasp of its methods, is not the view of the properly trained sociologist; for the characteristic of the sociologist, as distinct from the ordinary historian, is that he applies the methods of modern science to the study of human society. He regards sociology as the latest-born of the sciences, and so regarding it he necessarily accepts as valid, speaking broadly, the methods and conclusions of the other sciences and the general view of human thought and its objects which the modern sciences in the aggregate, when systematised by philosophy, are found to involve or suggest. And therefore, it may be said, he does not and cannot come to the scientific study of the history of belief as a social fact, without any other criterion than sociology itself affords: he necessarily has in his mind, whether implicitly or explicitly, the view of truth and its criteria which follows from assuming the general truth of the conclusions of the established and recognised sciences, and the validity of their methods—as to which there is no longer any general dispute or doubt among educated persons. He does not, of course, assume that these sciences are free from error, or that the human intellect has reached finality even in the most advanced of them: but he does assume that, in the vast region of thought covered by them, the human mind has found out the right way, after trying wrong ways: and consequently in forecasting the future development of thought he assumes that there will be no such fundamental changes as have taken place in the long struggle through error to truth which history shows us in the past. Making these assumptions, he finds in the history of thought a progress towards truth and knowledge; and thinks himself justified in inferring, with more or less confidence, that the progress will continue in the future. But he forecasts this progress differently, according as it is conceived to relate (1) to the sciences or systems of thought which have already emerged from the state of fundamental controversy, or (2) to those other parts of our thought that are still imperfectly organised, still struggling with fundamental controversies. As regards the former, the progress that may be expected will more or less resemble that which has taken place in them in the latest, strictly modern stage of their past history: while in the case of the latter—to which Ethics and Politics belong—the progress may be expected to imitate more or less the earlier struggle.

It is in this way, as we before saw, that Auguste Comte obtains his generalisations as to the 'three stages' through which a science has to pass: according to him, the sciences now clearly established are so because they have arrived at the 'positive' stage, after passing through the 'theological' and 'metaphysical' stages. At the positive stage they confine themselves to investigating the laws of phenomena; whereas at the theological stage, in a vain pursuit of the causes of events, they referred them to the volitions of imaginary quasi-human beings, and at the metaphysical stage, carrying on the same vain pursuit, they referred them to occult incognisable substances or essences. In the physical sciences then, these vain pursuits are now abandoned : whereas politics, he says, is still partly in the metaphysical stage, so far as its reasonings are based on the conception of certain abstract rights; while ethics is even still further back in the theological stage. He draws, therefore, from history the simple lesson that these backward studies should follow the course of development of the more successful physical sciences and become positive in their method.

You observe that Comte uses the terms 'theological' and 'metaphysical' to denote not spheres of legitimate inquiry, but forms of error : and that the error is twofold : in either case questions are asked which it is vain to ask, and also answers are given which there is no warrant for giving. The error in questioning was in the attempt to know realities and their causes, instead of acquiescing in the knowable limitations which restrict us to the knowledge of phenomena and their laws.

This doctrine, therefore, combines a belief in the Relativity of knowledge, in the philosophical sense, with a belief in the Progress of knowledge : and in Comte's view the combination is fundamentally important. Still the combination is in no way necessary : in fact the majority of scientific men hold with Comte that our knowledge at the present day is essentially and vastly in advance of what was taken for knowledge in preceding ages, without also holding that we cannot know realities.

§ 3. We may thus, then, pass from a consideration of what I called Relativism to a consideration of what I called Progressivism, the doctrine that the changes which history shows us in the prevalent beliefs of, let us say, our own society, exhibit a progress from less to more of knowledge and truth.

Now here I ought to say at once, that of the truth of this doctrine, in a broad and general sense, I have no doubt. And speaking broadly we may say that there is no doubt of it in the mind of our age. The extremest scepticism, at the present day, is limited by a belief in the validity of the methods and conclusions of physical science, which carries with it a belief in the steady growth of physical knowledge. This is a fundamental difference between the thought of our age and that not merely of the ancient world, but of a time so near us as the age of Descartes. When Descartes, at the outset of his independent investigation of truth, cleared his mind of many traditional and doubtful matters, he seems to have had no more difficulty in clearing out traditional physical science than anything else. But for a modern thinker any similar clearance — except as a conscious methodological artifice — would be forced and insincere. The question for us is not whether there has been progress in the attainment of truth in the study of the physical world: it can only be either (1) as to the nature and limits of this progress, or (2) as to the validity of the inferences drawn from it, in respect of knowledge generally, and especially of the prospects and means of progress in other departments.

These questions I propose to consider in the next lecture. At present it seems to me desirable, as a preliminary, to examine the notion of Progress rather from a sociological point of view. From a philosophical point of view, we might concentrate attention on progress in knowledge; but from the sociological point of view we have to consider this special kind of progress in relation to progress in society generally. Now of these two notions it is obvious the narrower —progress in knowledge—is comparatively simple and clear: at least any serious student of whatever subject knows what it is to acquire new knowledge and to get rid of errors and confusions of thought in his old knowledge—or what he took for such. But the wider notion 'social progress,' though no less familiar, is, in ordinary thought, much vaguer. An American poet, in verses whose popularity shows the effectiveness of the appeal, gives it as the fundamental duty of man

> . . . to act that each to-morrow
> Find us further than to-day.

But 'further' towards what? I am inclined to think that not a few enthusiasts for Progress might with truth adopt the frank declaration of another transatlantic bard, who tells his fellow-men and readers:

> I have urged you forward and still urge you—
> Without the slightest idea of our destination.

Let us then first try to get as clear as we can the wider notion of social progress, as preliminary to an examination of the narrower notion of progress in knowledge or the possession of truth.

We may first make the notion more distinct by excluding the old idea of a periodic or cyclical course of changes, for which however, as I would show if I had time, the facts of history give some support, especially in the succession of forms of polity.[1] But even where the notion of a recurring series of changes is most in harmony with the facts, it never corresponds to more than one part or aspect of the facts: the later series always differs from the earlier, to which it bears some analogy, in characteristics of great and fundamental importance;[2] the question therefore remains whether, so far as we consider the course of social change in its non-periodic aspect, we find progress in it, and what progress.

Now in ordinary thought and life we are in the habit of conceiving progress as movement towards an end which is ultimately attained, so that the progress can be measured simply by diminishing distance from the end. Thus in any journey we make progress till we arrive at our destination; so in most definite pieces of work—building a house, writing a book, etc.—the conception of progress is inseparable from the anticipation of completion and attainment, an anticipation which is normally realised: the house gets built, the

---

[1] For example, the evolution of the West European Country-state in medieval and modern history has some remarkable analogies to the evolution of the Greek City-state in old Græco-Roman history.

[2] For example, in making the comparison suggested in the previous note, we have to observe the great differences due to slavery, monotheistic religion, development of industry, etc.

book gets written, and the series of progressive changes comes to an end with the complete attainment of the planned result.

Now a similar notion seems to me very commonly applied, with more or less distinctness, in current discourses and schemes of political and social progress. The party of progress conceive a condition of things— a new distribution of political power, or a new distribution of wealth, or perhaps universal peace, or all these together—which they hope to realise, if not within their own lifetime, at any rate within a period comparatively short when measured in relation to the whole life of human society; and they conceive the realisation of this condition as giving so much satisfaction that the present political and social movement and unrest will cease and social *repose* follow—the repose of a social mind satisfied. But history gives no support to this notion; at least, the satisfaction and repose attained by any movement of political and social change in the past have never been more than partial and transient; and there is no reason to think it will be otherwise in the future.

I think, therefore, that, if we are to have a practically useful notion of social progress, we must not take the conception of a condition to be realised in which the progress is to *terminate* and the 'repose of a mind satisfied' to be won, as inseparable from the notion of progress. And indeed when we consider the deepest aims of a purposeful human life, we find that a notion of progress, quite apart from any hoped-for arrival at rest or termination of movement, is familiar at least to thoughtful persons. Thus a man of moral aspirations aims at progress in virtue, a man of intellectual aspirations at progress in knowledge, but in neither case is there any termination to the progress even hoped for, at least in earthly life; no one hopes to become perfectly virtuous or to attain complete knowledge. The pursuit of virtue, he knows, is one in which he can only arrive, by the utmost effort, at a somewhat closer approximation to an ideal which he can never hope actually to attain. Indeed the pursuit is, often at least, like a climb in which 'Alps on Alps arise,' since in proportion as a man's moral consciousness is developed, he feels the gap between his actual conduct and his ideal of conduct: he sees more clearly what he might have been and done, and how unlike it is to what he has been and done. And much the same may be said of knowledge: those who know most are those who see most clearly how much remains unknown; how on all sides round the small island of known fact which the human mind possesses, there stretches a vast, vague ocean of the unknown—not to speak of the pools and marshes and bottomless pits of error which are from time to time discovered in the island itself. Progress, in short, in virtue or in knowledge, as the experience of the individual declares, is progress towards an ideal more and more distinctly recognised to be beyond attainment, though we may advance in the direction of it.

But it still remains to ask what is the direction of progress? If, as our poet says, we are 'to act that each to-morrow find us further than to-day' from the point at which our progress began, what is—to use our poet's words—the 'destined end or goal' towards which the progress is tending, even if we may never expect to reach it? Now here a distinction of meanings or applications in the notion 'End' comes into view. There are no less than *three* such meanings, *primâ facie* distinct, all of which naturally come into this investigation :—(1) We may accept—with certain qualifications—the view of Society as an organism. This implies that there is adjustment or adaptation of the different elements of the aggregate social structure to the preservation of the organism under its conditions of existence. The 'End' therefore, in a sense, of the adaptation or adjustment is the preservation of the organism: that is, it is a result which each particular adaptation or adjustment attains in some measure—otherwise we should not call it adaptation or adjustment. (2) But in this sense 'End' is not necessarily to be regarded as a goal or ultimate result, towards which the series of changes are a progress, or which they are progressively realising: just as those who have affirmed that his own happiness is always the end of an individual man's striving have not intended to affirm that happiness is progressively realised in the series of changes that constitutes the life of the individual. Nor again does the 'End,' as meaning the preservation of the organism, give us any clue to the direction in which the series of self-adaptive changes is tending; for it is simply a common characteristic of all organisms, in fact what constitutes their essentially organic character, that organic change has this tendency; while (3) the result to which, according to Sociological inquiry, we seem to be probably tending may be different from what our reason approves as an ethical or political end—an end which we ought to aim at realising.

Meaning then by 'End,' as implied in the term 'organism,' that the complex structure and mutually dependent functions of the parts of an organism are adapted or adjusted to the attainment of a certain result, namely, the preservation of the organism under its conditions of existence, are we to understand that social progress lies in the increase of this adaptation or adjustment, in the fact that the structure of the society becomes continually more adapted to preserve itself under the conditions of its existence? There can be no doubt that an important part of the changes which history shows us have the character of being such adaptations to meet changes in internal or external conditions. But this alone does not justify us in concluding that the social organism is on the whole progressing in self-preservative qualities: as the changes within and without it may be unfavourable to its preservation to an extent that may outweigh the advantages of the adaptive changes. We may find instances of political changes, which though they may undoubtedly be regarded as self-adaptive alterations of the political society in which they occur, cannot be shown to have given the particular society in question or its type an increased prospect of self-preservation. Consider for instance the political changes to which I just now referred when mentioning the general notion of cyclical or periodic movement.[1] The movement towards popular government which appears to begin in Greece in the seventh century, seems to be due to a combination of causes, including a movement of political thought of which I will speak presently. But without at present analysing the causes of the movement, or distinguishing its nobler and baser elements, we may say that neither observation of its nature, nor a general survey of its historic effects would lead us to regard it as being decidedly a preservative adaptation of the political societies in which it is realised. Certainly no Greek observer conceived democracy to be for the advantage of a Greek city-state in the struggle for existence: and in medieval Italy it is the Venetian oligarchy, and not any more popular constitution, which seems to stand first in the possession of self-preservative qualities.

And the same may be said of the other changes which, taken together, make up what we commonly conceive as 'progress in civilisation': *i.e.* the development of the arts of industry, and of the fine arts, including literature, and developments of habits of peaceful and orderly living, both of which co-operate in increasing mutual communication among human beings and so in causing an extension of sociality and sympathy. In two ways, indeed, this group of more or less connected changes is socially preservative; so far as it increases the power of the society and its

[1] Cf. above, p. 198 *n*.

members to adapt their physical environment to the satisfaction of their needs and desires, and so far as it increases the internal cohesion of the society through the repression of disorderly violence and the expansion of sympathy. On the other hand, so far as the development of habits of peaceful industry and trade tends to unfit its members, physically or morally, for war and martial exercises, it is a dangerous source of weakness in conflicts with other social groups. Indeed history shows us several striking instances of the conquest of more civilised states by less civilised, owing to the superiority of the latter in fighting qualities. The most impressive example, for Europeans, is the conquest of the Western Empire by the Teutonic tribes. It was a main cause of this event that the civilised Roman provincial did not like fighting, and the barbarian did: so that the armies of the Empire came to be more and more composed of barbarians, who were thus trained and disciplined for the civilised 'art of war': until the time came when the overwhelming preponderance of fighting force possessed by the Teutonic tribes, inside and outside the imperial armies, was too palpable a fact to be effectually obscured by the traditional prestige of the Roman state and the politic skill of the Roman governing class.

It would seem, then, that at any rate a very important part of the changes which history shows us in human societies have no marked tendency to make them more adapted to self-preservation under the conditions of their existence.

§ 4. Let us now turn from the general question that we have been considering to examine the special case of changes in prevalent beliefs—with which, in this course of lectures, I am specially concerned.

It must be observed that the notion of 'progress' in this special department is likely to be understood —even by sociologists—in what I have regarded as its philosophical rather than its primarily sociological meaning: *i.e.* as progress in *truth*, either in respect of extent of truth known or of freedom from error. Such a progress we all accept as a fact in some departments at least: but, as I have already argued at some length, the sociologist pure and simple has no scientific right to assume it with regard to beliefs in general. For he cannot assume it without at the same time assuming implicitly a criterion of truth in general: and such a criterion it is the primary business of philosophy, not of sociology as such, to establish. If we keep strictly to the sociological point of view, we shall properly consider 'progress' as applied to changes in beliefs as a special case of the general notion of social progress: and the question we shall primarily raise with regard to such changes will be not whether a given series of changes historically surveyed is in the direction of truth, but whether it is in the direction of expediency for the social organism, whether it tends continually to increase the social organism's power of preserving itself under the conditions of its existence. This is the primary question prescribed by the changes in prevalent beliefs from a sociological point of view;

and—for a reason that will appear hereafter—it is important to examine it separately from the question as to the tendency of such changes in the direction of truth.

Let us ask then how far we can reasonably regard the general process of social adaptation to the environment—especially through the struggle for existence among societies and the survival of the fittest society—as having operated to bring into existence beliefs tending to the preservation of the society.

Certainly this last cause may be held in prehistoric times to have tended to promote the increase of knowledge of natural phenomena, through the increased means of supplying human wants which attends it. 'Necessity is the mother of invention,' and invention depends on observation and forecast of natural facts; and industrial inventions are, speaking broadly, conducive to the preservation of the society in which they occur and may be assumed to have given inventive societies an advantage in the struggle for existence with other societies: though as inventions spread through imitation, the advantage would be proportionally shared by imitative neighbours. And we can conceive that natural selection among societies may have similarly operated to keep in existence religious beliefs conducive to social preservation in primitive ages. For example, if ancestor worship led to energetic and harmonious co-operation, then the tribe that did not worship its ancestors, becoming slack and quarrelsome, would be so much the more likely to be conquered by the ancestor worshippers.

But we cannot reasonably regard this as the sole or even the main part of the explanation of the movement of beliefs even in primitive ages: because it is obviously a cause that has no great effect as regards the important changes in beliefs known to have taken place in the historic period. For no civilised society, in the historic development of European civilisation, has suffered destruction such that its beliefs died with it. Take the case of Greece: it may be suggested that the philosophic criticism of current polytheism, by which—as we perceive from Greek literature—the influence of religion on the sentiments of cultivated society was weakened, made the Greek States somewhat weaker in the struggle for political existence. Now let us suppose for the sake of argument—it would be a fantastic hypothesis—that this was so in the struggle with Rome, and that the Romans had an important advantage in being more genuinely attached to their deities. Still Greek polity did not perish in any sense which made Greek beliefs perish: as we all know, it was quite the contrary—

> Græcia capta ferum victorem cepit.

So again if we turn to the momentous change of beliefs effected in the second and third centuries of our era, the struggle for existence among political societies has obviously no effect in bringing it about. It is within the region subject to settled and stable Roman dominion that the change goes on.

Nor is there indeed any adequate evidence that the historic changes in religious beliefs have had any general tendency to preserve the particular societies in which they occurred from the only kind of death which historically known human societies have had seriously to dread—destruction by foreign enemies. Take the case last mentioned. I see no reason to think that Christianity had a preservative effect on the Roman Empire. Probably before Constantine, its operation was the other way. As we know, in the view of primitive Christians, ordinary human society was a world temporarily surrendered to Satanic rule, over which a swift and sudden destruction was impending: the passive alienation from secular work and aims, and the decline of patriotic sentiment which this view carried with it, could hardly fail to be a source of weakness and danger to the political system: indeed we may attribute the Decian persecutions largely to a sense of this growing danger. The action of Constantine, again, was no doubt largely determined by a desire to heal the split between religion and the state: and this was certainly a political advantage. But apart from the removal of this drawback and danger caused by the spread of Christianity, it is difficult to see that Christianity after Constantine had any preservative efficacy for Roman political society: the Empire seems to be steadily declining in the fourth and fifth centuries.

No doubt, in the social chaos to which the barbarian invasions reduced the Western Empire, the Church was of great value to civilisation as a source of unity to the whole West-European State-system —though of disintegration sometimes to particular states. When the Empire broke up, the Church held together and held Western Europe together. But it is the vigorous *community* of belief that had this binding force, rather than its specifically Christian character.

Observe, I am not disputing the general value— even the indispensability—of religion as a social force. I am only arguing that when we examine, from a purely sociological point of view, the changes in religious beliefs, with the view of ascertaining the laws of change, we can find no evidence in the historic period of a clear general tendency in these changes to promote the preservation of the social organism in which they take place; and have therefore no adequate ground for assuming such a general tendency in the primitive period.

Somewhat the same may be said of changes in political beliefs—beliefs as to what ought to be in the structure of government and its relations to the governed—so far as history shows us such changes. No doubt political beliefs are strongly influenced by the struggles for existence of the societies in which they are prevalent. Thus beliefs hostile to existing political order tend to diminish in crises of national struggle with other nations, from the strongly felt advantage of internal harmony and cohesion. A war, at least of defence, strengthens the position of rulers whose military management is successful: on the other hand, reverses in war favour the growth of beliefs hostile to government. But though, in tracing the history of political beliefs, this is an influence not to be neglected, it cannot be said to give the main law of their development. Consider, for instance, the change in political ideas which, as I have said, has —more than once, in human history—preceded and partly caused the transition to democracy. The causes are surely to be sought in the general desire of human beings as individuals to better their condition, and enjoy a larger share of the means of happiness, co-operating with the ethico-political conviction that any man—or any freeman—has as much right as any other to determine how the matters of common interest should be carried on. This movement, wisely directed and moderated, may, no doubt, strengthen the political society in which it takes place for international struggles; but certainly history does not show a general tendency to this result: the experience of Greece seems rather to have been that it had a preponderantly disintegrative effect, producing, as Plato says, "two hostile states—the rich and the poor —within the limits of one."

I turn now to an objection which may have long since occurred to my readers. "You have been talking," it may be said, "all along of Preservation of Society as the end of adaptations, and of increase in self-preservative qualities as the essence of progress. But surely Preservation alone, bare continuance of existence, is not a worthy end; nor does this represent our idea of progress, nor is the contemplation of it capable of stirring the springs of political and social activity. This is aimed not at mere Being, but Well-being. By progress, we mean improvement, the passage from a worse to a better condition. Political beliefs—at any rate at the present stage of development of civilised Society—are beliefs as to what ought to be done, in the organisation and functioning of government, to bring about a better condition of society; and the interesting question in any general study of history, in order to ascertain the law of development, is how far things are tending to *improvement* of social life." In all this I entirely agree: and have only appeared to ignore it so far from a desire to keep strictly to the sociological point of view. If we introduce the notion of 'improvement,' and insist on thinking with method and precision, we require some definite criterion and measure of 'good.'

LECTURE XI

RELATION OF PHILOSOPHY TO SOCIOLOGY (*continued*)

§ 1. IN my last lecture I passed from a consideration of the Sociological view of the divergent beliefs of different ages and stages of social evolution, which I distinguished as Relativism, to examine the other view, which I distinguished as Progressivism. As I explained, in distinguishing the two I have by no means intended to imply that the two views are necessarily opposed. In fact they are not only capable of being held together, but probably the commonest form of Relativism is combined with and modified by Progressivism: that is to say, it is the view that the fundamental beliefs of our ancestors, so far as divergent from our own—in such subjects as Ethics, Politics, and Sociology—were, speaking broadly, 'relatively' true; but yet less true, a more remote approximation to truth, than our own.

But I have thought it best, for clearness, to examine the two views separately: to conceive the Progressivists as holding the simple doctrine that the history of mankind shows us a more or less constant progress in knowledge: and to examine the exact nature of the progress, and the epistemological inferences to be drawn from it. I conceive that the doctrine cannot be regarded as purely sociological nor as attained by a purely sociological method, but rather by a combination of Sociology with Philosophy: as it involves the assumption of a criterion to distinguish true knowledge from false, which Sociology alone cannot assume.

Further, it seemed to me desirable, before examining progress in knowledge, to consider the wider notion of Social Progress from a purely Sociological point of view. I began by pointing out that the general notion of Social progress does not necessarily imply an expected or even a possible arrival at a final condition of Society as a goal and termination of the progressive movement; but only increase in certain definite characteristics of the social organism now possessed in some degree. Now as the common conception of the social organism implies adaptation of its structure and the functioning of its different organs to preservation of the organism under its conditions of existence, it is natural to understand Progress as meaning progress in self-preservative quality. But an examination of the facts of history seemed to show that historically ascertained changes in human society have certainly no universal tendency to increase the efficiency of the organism for self-preservation: and, in particular, that the historically ascertained changes in beliefs have no such general tendency.

I then passed to observe that, in any case, the notion of 'increase in self-preservative quality' does not correspond to the generally current notion of social progress, which involves the idea of *improvement*: *i.e.* increase in well-being and not merely of mere life and promise of further life, apart from any regard to the quality of the life.

§ 2. But if we introduce the notion of 'Improvement' and insist on thinking with method and precision, we require some definite criterion and measure of 'good.' And this, I conceive, it belongs to Practical Philosophy to establish: it is not a matter with which Sociology pure and simple has *primâ facie* any concern. So long as we confine ourselves to the system of notions which have been transferred from Biology to Sociology—and which seem, at present at least, to be an indispensable stock-in-trade of the latter science —the notions of organism, adaptation or adjustment, differentiation and correlation of parts, mutual dependence of co-ordinated functions, etc.—it seems to me that the end to which reference is made in all these notions is not Happiness but Preservation. Sociological writers sometimes veil this from their readers by the use of the ambiguous terms 'social health' and 'social welfare'; for these, in ordinary thought, carry with them, more or less distinctly, the implication of general happiness as an effect of the 'health' and at least an element of the 'welfare': but I conceive that, interpreted in a strict biological or sociological sense, 'health' or 'welfare' of organisms can only mean self-preservative conditions of structure and correlated functions tending to self-preservation. If we take 'social welfare' interpreted in any other sense than that of preservative conditions as the end and standard by which progress is estimated, we do so on other than biological or sociological grounds.

At the same time, I think that Sociology itself ultimately forces us beyond what I have called the primary sociological conception of social progress; on account of the divergence—widening, as our examination proceeds—between progress of civilisation as commonly conceived and increase in qualities tending to the preservation of the particular social organism in which the progress occurs. A consideration of this divergence will lead us, I think, to two conclusions. First, even if we confine our attention, in considering social progress, to a particular political society, we must—if we would maintain harmony with Common Sense—find a wider conception of the criterion of progress than is afforded by the mere notion of conduciveness to social preservation. For we cannot but recognise that the development of sociality and polite order, of knowledge and the arts of peace—in particular of the fine arts and literature—is a good thing for a society, even though it does not render it more capable of preserving itself under the actual conditions of its environment, physical and social: it is a gain, so far as it goes, though the gain may in a particular case be outweighed by the loss of fighting quality. And secondly, we cannot, without doing violence to our deepest convictions, consider this gain *only* in relation to the particular society whose progress we are contemplating: we must also consider it in relation to humanity at large. For the gain of the complex fact that we call civilisation is something that is not normally confined to the particular society in which it first takes place: it tends to spread by imitation and tradition to contemporary societies and to societies that are to live in later ages, so that its most striking achievements become possessions of a continually larger part of the human race. And thus, as we come down the stream of time, we are led irresistibly to pass from the point of view of Mr. Spencer's Sociology—which treats different human groups as separate organisms, like animals or plants—to the point of view of Comte's Sociology, which by preference conceives "the whole human race, past and future, as constituting a vast and eternal social unit." Putting these two considerations together we cannot, I think, measure social progress by any narrower conception than that of conduciveness to the welfare of humanity at large.

§ 3. But, it may be asked, how are we to obtain a true and adequately precise conception of social welfare and the means of realising it: since history shows us variation and diversity in this conception as well as in other fundamental conceptions and principles of Ethics and Politics? This question leads us back to the discussion of the claim of Sociology[1]—not alone but with the help of a certain epistemological assumption, to establish a criterion of truth and error and, by the aid of this criterion, to present the series of changes in prevalent beliefs which history shows us as steps in a progress towards fuller and purer truth.

[1] Cf. above, Lect. X. § 2.

I will first again state this claim in what seems to me its most plausible form. It may be said :—Granting that a study of the history of beliefs cannot by itself furnish a criterion of their truth, still the comparative historical study of different departments of systematic thought may furnish a criterion of practical value, provided we accept the general validity of systems of thought which any instructed person can see to have finally emerged from the condition of fundamental controversy, and such are the established and recognised sciences. For whatever theoretical defects the subtlety of sceptical philosophers may detect in the fundamental assumptions and methods of modern Astronomy, Physics, Chemistry, Physiology, no one— not even a philosopher—doubts that they really are sciences. They are not, of course, complete and perfect bodies of knowledge, probably not even quite free from error as far as they go. Still, they are established sufficiently for practical purposes by the decisive tests of (1) Agreement of Experts—the acceptance of the same principles, methods, and conclusions by the overwhelming majority of serious students throughout the civilised world, and (2) Continuity of Development —the manner in which the new truths continually discovered fit into and confirm the old. Accepting these sciences, then, as' types of real knowledge and right method, we may use them as models by which to correct and improve the remaining parts of the aggregate of prevalent beliefs : by studying the development of these successfully organised bodies of thought, we may learn to develop rightly those other parts of our thought that are still imperfectly organised, still struggling with fundamental doubts and controversies. This, then, it may be said, is what Sociology does: this is how it aids the philosopher to find a practical solution of the difficulties of his search for a criterion of truth.

It is in this way, as we saw, that Comte obtains his generalisation—of which I before spoke—as to the 'three stages' through which, in any department, the pursuit of knowledge has to pass. According to him, as I have said, the sciences now clearly established are so because they have arrived at the 'positive' stage, after passing through the theological and metaphysical stages; whereas politics is still partly in the metaphysical stage, and ethics even lingering in the theological. He therefore concludes that ethics and politics—following the course of development of the more advanced sciences—will eventually become 'positive' in their method, that is, become branches or applications of Sociology. Sociology thus allies itself with the pre-existing sciences, confirms their claims to be bodies of real knowledge, and taking them, as it were, under its wing, claims in unison with them an exclusive right of deciding as to truth and falsehood on all matters of interest to man: Theology and Metaphysics being relegated to the position of different stages of error, through which the human mind progresses in its advance towards truth.

Now I do not dispute the general reasonableness and utility of the kind of comparison which Comte indicates and exemplifies: I agree with him in the importance he attaches to *consensus* (of different minds) and *coherence* (of beliefs of the same mind) as tests of truth. I do not say that they are infallible tests; but they are the best that I can find, in the case of a prevalent belief that does not present itself as self-evident to me: and as men have erred in apparently intuitive judgments, 'consensus' of experts and coherence with other beliefs are important supplementary securities, even for apparently self-evident beliefs. So far my methodology agrees with Comte's. I am even disposed to admit a large element of truth in his doctrine of three stages so far as it is positive: only instead of 'Theology' and 'Metaphysics' I should venture to substitute 'crude theology' and 'bad metaphysics.' To this I shall return presently.

The fundamental controversies in politics and ethics turn mainly on the definition of a single fundamental principle. They relate to the *ultimate end*, which gives the standard by which all particular rules and institutions are to be tested. Thus at present it is a subject of active philosophical controversy whether this end is Happiness, an aggregate of pleasures realised in successive parts of time in the lives of individuals; or whether it is some Universal Good which is the good of each because it is the good of all, and not the good of all by the summation of the goods of individuals. Our reasoning to particular conclusions, ethical or political, must be fundamentally different, according as we adopt one or other of these alternatives, but I cannot see how the subject of controversy can be treated at all by a 'positive' instead of a metaphysical method. Ultimate ends are not 'phenomena' or laws or conditions of phenomena: to investigate them as if they were seems as futile as if one inquired whether they were square or round.

It may be replied that a study of the established sciences, as recognised by agreement of experts and continuity of development, will at any rate aid us in deciding general questions of method—*e.g.* whether the mind, to attain sound systematic knowledge, should begin with the universal and proceed downwards to the particular, or *vice versâ*. Now if it were established, as some thinkers hold, that all sciences begin with and rest upon universal intuitions or postulates, or again, as others hold, that they all start from and are based upon cognitions of particular facts, or, thirdly, that they all combine universal and particular knowledge in the same manner and degree, we might infer with some probability that our reasonings as to what ought to be should be formed on the same type. But these points are notoriously subjects of controversy on which we cannot decide without entering deep into the metaphysics that Comte repudiates. If we take the established sciences simply so far as they are cognisable as a social fact—*i.e.* so far as their method is allowed to be beyond the range of controversy—we find in them diversity, not identity of methods: in some cases the premises, reasonings, and conclusions are all universal (mathematics): in others all the generalisations attained are admittedly based on particular experiences and tested by agreement with these. Thus a survey of the sciences does not even provide us with a decided analogy to aid us in our discussion of ultimate practical ends: it gives no clear guidance beyond the general direction to aim at bringing our ethical and political judgments—so far as they relate to ultimate good and evil—into systematic harmony and agreement.

My general conclusion, then, is that Sociology cannot be accepted as a substitute for Philosophy, in the task of co-ordinating beliefs; nay, further, though the study of beliefs from a strictly sociological point of view must always be of great interest for philosophy, the aid given by Sociology in the special problem of establishing and applying valid criteria of truth and error must always be of a subordinate kind.

§ 4. Let us turn to consider Comte's Law of the three Stages. And here I have taken for granted that we are all prepared to assume broadly the validity of modern science and its methods, and surveying the past history of thought with this assumption, to recognise that the human mind, after many centuries of tentative and confused inquiry, after traversing many devious ways of thought, has found the right method of dealing with the physical world, the world of sensible experience, and has now, for some time, been making clear, steady, and continuous progress. The question is, what inference we are to draw from this conclusion as to the matters with which Theology and Metaphysics deal. The inference drawn not only by Comte, but also by Mr. Spencer, is, as we know, sweeping and negative. According to Comte Sociology, assuming the validity of the modern sciences, and tracing their progressive history, establishes the generalisation of the three stages through which human thought has to pass, and thus effectually antiquates Theology and Metaphysics. And though Mr. Spencer's Philosophy, as well as his Sociology, differs most importantly from Comte's, he agrees with him, as we have seen, in affirming—as the outcome of the long process of human thought—that the Reality which it has been for thousands of years the central aim of Theology and Metaphysics to know is totally and for ever unknowable, and that the only positive work of Philosophy is to systematise the sciences and to comprehend their generalisations in a higher generalisation.

Let us examine first the claim to antiquate Theology. As Mill says, what Comte calls the Theological explanation of the facts of nature might perhaps be more clearly designated the Personal or Volitional explanation of them. It regards the facts of the universe as determined by the volitions of unseen beings, with quasi-human wills. It is therefore in Comte's view opposed to science, whose progressive work has consisted in exhibiting these facts as governed by invariable laws of existence and sequence: and, as we trace the growth of human knowledge, we find the Theological explanation continually receding and fading in successive departments of inquiry, as the scientific explanation establishes itself.

We need not trace the process in detail: the broad truth of this historical generalisation is, I conceive, undeniable. The Theological view has thus opposed the scientific, in modern no less than in ancient times, and has had continually to give way and retire before the triumphant onward march of science. But when we look closer at the opposition, we find that the conflict arises in one of two ways; and in neither case is it fundamental and inevitable. Theology has been opposed to science, so far as it has conceived its divinities as beings with capricious, irregular volitions, moved by anger and favour, and—when the divinities are conceived as many—liable to conflict: and it has also been opposed to science so far as it conceives the divine volitions to be inscrutable. In the former case it has come into conflict with the conclusions of scientific inquiry, the system of invariable laws which this inquiry, so far as successful, has steadily unfolded: in the latter case it has come into conflict with the freedom of inquiry which the progress of science demands. But it is obvious that the one opposition vanishes as soon as the Divine Will is conceived as a Will in which there is no caprice or irregularity, 'no variableness, neither shadow of turning'; and the other vanishes as soon as the Divine Will is conceived as a Will whose order may without limit be investigated by human minds: and both these conceptions are now almost, if not quite, established in the minds of most educated persons.

It may be said, however, that the removal of these oppositions only reveals a deeper opposition between the universal order that Science presents, and the universal order that Theology claims to present. For the order that science presents to us, the system of invariable laws that it discovers in the process of continual change, is, when we apply to it our human conceptions of good and evil, not a perfectly good order. *Primâ facie*, indeed, these categories appear irrelevant to it: and accordingly, leading men of science have declared that nature as known by science is non-ethical, and that the whole moral effort of mankind to modify nature must be recognised as an effort to which Nature—if I may so say—is indifferent. But I need not now dwell on this view, since (1) it is not obviously supported by history, and (2) it is certainly not the practical view of our leading Sociologists : their forecast of the future of society is always a forecast of social life growing better through the operation of sociological laws. Indeed in Mr. Spencer's view it is a future so bright that I am obliged regretfully to point out that its roseate hues are palpably not warranted by the knowledge we possess of past biological and sociological evolution. But in any case the world of science remains, from an ethical point of view, an imperfect world. The result worked out by its invariable laws is a chequered result of good mixed with evil; and therefore though it may present no obstacle to the conception of an orderly will as the cause and ground of the process that it has partially come to understand, it still does profoundly oppose the conception of a perfectly good will.

But this is not all. There is a deeper opposition than that arising from the imperfection with which good is realised in the world as made known to us by science. It is said that the system of laws which the sciences show us is a system which, though it may not be strictly incompatible with the theological conception of an orderly will, still in no way supports this conception and tends to its exclusion: since it gives us an order intelligible indeed, and so in a sense rational, but one from which the conceptions of the Practical Reason—the conceptions of End, Design, Adaptation of Means to End—are excluded.

§ 5. On this I may first remark that if the scientific view of the Universe is thus opposed to current Theology, it is equally opposed to Metaphysics, so far as Metaphysics deals with what I called the central and fundamental problem of reconciling Theoretical and Practical Philosophy. And this leads me to say a few words on Comte's conception—substantially accepted by Mill—of the Metaphysical view of nature which he supposes to oust the Theological view, and to intervene between that and the scientific view. According to Comte (I give a brief summary in Mill's words): "In this [the metaphysical] stage it is no longer a god that causes and directs the various agencies of nature: it is a power, or a force, or an occult quality, considered as real existences, inherent in but distinct from the concrete bodies in which they reside. . . . Instead of Dryads presiding over trees, . . . every plant or animal has now a Vegetative Soul, the $\theta\rho\epsilon\pi\tau\iota\kappa\dot{\eta}$ $\psi\upsilon\chi\dot{\eta}$ of Aristotle. At a later period the Vegetative Soul has become a Plastic Force, and still later, a Vital Principle. Objects now do all that they do because it is their Essence to do so, or by reason of an inherent Virtue." Again, "phenomena are accounted for by supposed tendencies and propensities of the abstraction Nature. . . . The rise of water in a pump is attributed to Nature's horror of a vacuum. The fall of heavy bodies, and the ascent of flame and smoke are construed as attempts of each to get to its *natural* place. Many important consequences are deduced from the doctrine that Nature has no leaps or breaks of continuity: and 'in medicine' reparative processes in the organism are referred to the *vis medicatrix* of Nature."[1]

Now no doubt this kind of illusory explanation of physical facts, by referring them to occult essences, qualities, forces, and natural tendencies, has occupied an important place in the historic efforts of the human mind to understand the physical world. And so far as it is derived, as it largely is derived, from Aristotle, there is a sense in which it may be called metaphysical: *i.e.* it may be attributed to the influence exercised by Aristotle's metaphysical system on his study of the physical world; and in part at least to a want of clear separation between metaphysical and physical problems. At the same time Comte and Mill overlook the fact that these conceptions are not, in Aristotle's view, strictly metaphysical but physical: that is, they do not belong to that part of his philosophy—'First Philosophy' or Philosophy of Divine things—which relates to the eternal and unchanged, the Ground and End of the process of change and movement in the physical world. When we make

[1] J. S. Mill, *Auguste Comte and Positivism*, 1865, pp. 10, 11.

this distinction, it seems to me that Comte's conception of Metaphysics as a manner of thought that takes the place of the theological is superficial and inadequate; since a main aim and main effort of metaphysical speculation, in the post-Socratic Schools of Greece, was not to eliminate the theistic view of the universe as a whole, but to elevate and purify it. It thus served—especially no doubt in the Platonic and Stoic lines of thought, rather than the Aristotelian—as a positive preparation for Christian Monotheism: its importance did not lie merely in its negative and critical action in enfeebling Polytheism.

I should like to dwell further on this point, and especially to show the singular one-sidedness of Comte's historical judgment in regarding the change from Polytheism to Monotheism as importing a decline in the influence of religion upon human life. It is in a sense true that the presence of Divinity is withdrawn somewhat from the surface of human life, by the transition from Polytheism to Monotheism; but it is because it is withdrawn into the moral depths of life, not because its influence on life is weakened. But time presses, and I must return to the topic from which I digressed :—the alleged antiteleological tendency of modern science, which brings it into conflict, as I said, not only with current Theology, but with any form of Metaphysical Philosophy that retains the notion of End or Good as a fundamental conception in its system of the Universe—even though divorced from the conception of Personality.

In the first place, it seems to me that there is in

any case no collision between the inquiry, or body of systematic thought, which Theology has come to be, and any positive science or even the aggregate or system of such sciences. For a science, as Comte and his followers say, deals only with the existences and sequences of some department of the phenomena, of which the complex stream in time constitutes what we call the process of the world. And Science as a system does not profess to tell us anything of the First Cause of this whole process, its final end or significance, its underlying reality, and the relation to this of the human spirit, not as a mere series of phenomena or consciousnesses, but as the conscious, thinking, aspiring, self-determining subject of such a series. These, however, are the greater matters on which Theology or Metaphysics seeks or professes to give knowledge: their inquiries therefore move in a different region from that of positive Science, and no collision between the two is possible. They may even be regarded as mutually supplementary.

No doubt Theology or Constructive Metaphysics comes into collision with the Positive Philosophy: but then it comes into collision not with its systematisation of the sciences, but with its negative assertion that nothing can be known about the Universe except the laws of the existences and sequences of phenomena. And this negative assertion is just *not* a scientific conclusion: it is, in fact, a metaphysical dogma.

But, secondly, granting the antiteleological tendency of modern science, so far as it relates to the inorganic world, and even admitting this tendency as defensible in the sciences that deal with organic life, yet it cannot be admitted as such in the study of mind.

I think it noteworthy that the very development of thought which is supposed by Comte and his followers effectually to antiquate Theology — the development of Sociology as the culmination of positive science—should, according to Comte's own treatment of the method of Sociology, involve in a striking manner a kind of teleology: because he assumes that a real comprehension of earlier stages in development is only possible by viewing them in the light of later stages. For Comte insists on conceiving the society whose laws of development he traces as being humanity as a whole, a single social organism of which the different nations are organs. But we can only apply this conception to the earlier stages of social development by viewing them in the light thrown back on them by later stages. We can see on looking back that the Egyptians, the Greeks, the Romans were destined to be special organs of human progress; but even the sociologist could not have got this conception out of the facts some two or three thousand years ago. Similarly, in contemplating the fact on which Comtian Sociology lays most stress, in contemplating the most remarkable product of mind—scientific knowledge—in its latest stage, we find our thoughts carried forward rather than backward by the endeavour to comprehend its significance. We find ourselves irresistibly led to assume as real a completer knowledge, comprehending and going indefinitely beyond the imperfect and fragmentary knowledge possessed by human minds; and this inference is not—as in the case of arguments for Divine Design in the merely physical world—the introduction of a hypothesis *primâ facie* alien to the matter that we are studying. For these reasons, I think any admission of the antitheological tendency of modern science, in the way of discarding the 'celebrated argument from design,' should stop at the world of mind (including the world of animate life viewed on its mental side): and that when we concentrate attention on this world of mind, the tendency is rather the other way.

To sum up, I reject the claim of Sociology—or, as it is sometimes phrased, of the Historical method—to dominate our study of the problems of Philosophy, while fully admitting that the history of the laws of development of human society, and especially of human thought and belief, constitutes an important part of the knowledge that it is the business of Philosophy to systematise. I reject this claim in the form in which I admit it to be most plausible, namely, in that view of the history of thought which I have called Progressivism, which takes its stand on the admitted social fact of progress in knowledge, and especially points to the sciences which relate to the physical world as examples of right method attained after a long struggle through erroneous and confused methods. I reject it, partly on account of the diversity of methods which the different sciences, impartially viewed, are found to require and use :—the method of mathematics is most importantly different from that of abstract physics, the method of abstract physics different from that of the concrete study of the inorganic world, and this again different from that of the history of the world of life, while the methods of the studies of human life and thought, individual and social, are still tentative and beset with difficulties in which the analogy of the physical sciences can only give very limited assistance. I reject it, again, on account of the fundamental difference between the task of special sciences dealing with partial and limited aspects of the Universe and the task of Philosophy dealing with the Universe as a whole. In view of all these differences and difficulties, I conceive the one important lesson that Philosophy and Theology have to learn from the progress of Science is the vague lesson of patience and hope. Science sets before us an ideal of a consensus of experts and continuity of development which we may hope to attain in our larger and more difficult work.

LECTURE XII

RELATION OF THEORETICAL TO PRACTICAL PHILOSOPHY [1]

§ 1. IN this concluding lecture I have to attempt the consideration of the relation of Theoretical to Practical Philosophy, of our systematic knowledge—or what purports to be knowledge—of what is, has been, or will be—so far as we can forecast what will be—to our systematic knowledge, our system of reasoned judgments, as to what ought to be. In attempting this difficult problem, I think it best to simplify our task, by abstracting from any controversy or disagreement that exists within the range of Practical Philosophy. I assume, therefore, that we are agreed as to our methods of reasoning to practical conclusions, and that we have harmonised, in a manner that satisfies us, our judgments as to what ought to be. I do not assume our knowledge to be complete: there is no need of that, any more than there is any need of assuming completeness in our knowledge of the physical Universe. But I assume that it is coherent as far as it goes, that fundamental conflicts have been somehow settled.

[1] Cf. Prefatory Note.

I shall accordingly take what 'ought to be' to include what is commonly judged to be 'good,' so far as attainable by human action, as well as what is commonly judged to be 'right' or the duty of any human being. Of course 'Good' and 'Evil' as commonly used are wider and less stringent terms than 'Right' and 'Wrong'; since (1) the former are applicable to results out of reach of human attainment, *e.g.* an abundant harvest next autumn, or influenza in the winter; also (2) 'Goods' may be incompatible: to attain a greater we may have to sacrifice a less. But even when unattainable, or not preferable in the circumstances, what is judged to be 'good' would appear to have the same quality as the term imports within the range of its practical application: 'good' is the kind of thing that we 'ought' to seek to produce or maintain *pro tanto* and so far as it is in our power.

For simplicity I shall, at first, mean by 'good' in this discussion 'ultimate good on the whole'; good on the whole for human society, the world of living things, or the cosmos—whichever we take to be the larger whole of which the individual is a part, and which is conceived to have an ultimate good capable of being increased or diminished, promoted or retarded, by human action. In ethical discussion the notion of 'right' or 'duty' is, however, more familiar to the common moral consciousness of modern men than the notion of 'ultimate good.' But I shall assume it to be admitted by Common Sense that from the point of view of complete knowledge, the performance of a duty or a right act must be conceived to be either a part of ultimate good or a means to it.

Taking then the notion of Duty or Right act, I may assume it to be a continually recurrent element in the thought of an ordinary well-behaved person about his own life and that of others. In the thoughts of such men about duties, taken together and compared, there is doubtless more conflict and disagreement than in their thoughts about facts; but agreement much preponderates. Apart from such conflict, there is recognised a variation of duties from man to man; but it is commonly assumed that this variation rests on rational grounds, so that the duties of A, truly conceived, form one rationally coherent system with the duties of B. Such a system we may call a 'world of human duty,' of which each man conceives the duties he assigns to himself and his immediate neighbours to be a part indefinitely better known to him than the rest. But he conceives the whole world of duty to be a subject of human knowledge, no less than the world of fact; though the former is lamentably divergent from the latter, in consequence of the general failure of men, in a greater or less degree, to do their duty. The divergence is equally palpable if we consider the 'good' *results* that might be brought about by the performance of duty, as compared with what actually takes place. From either point of view we judge that 'what ought to be' to a great extent 'is not': and we commonly conceive that its character as 'what ought to be' is entirely independent of whether it comes into actual being or not.

§ 2. The question then is raised whether this distinction between what is and what ought to be is ultimate and irreducible? I think it rash to affirm irreducibility. Just as I would never say that anything is unknowable, but merely that it is unknown —for when we cannot answer a question it seems usually unwarrantable to assume that we understand the matter enough to prove the question unanswerable —so here I do not say that the difference of these notions is ultimately irreducible; but only that I am certainly not satisfied with any proposed reduction proceeding on the lines of scientific thought on which such reduction is commonly attempted. I do not think the desired result can be attained by considering moral judgments from a psychological or sociological point of view, as elements in the conscious life of individuals, or communities, or races. My grounds for this view I have already given in speaking of the relations of philosophy and sociology.[1] No doubt moral judgments and their accompanying sentiments are a department of psychical fact, and we may analyse and classify them as such, and investigate their causes, just as we should do in the case of any other psychical fact. But as long as they are regarded solely from this point of view, it seems impossible to explain or justify the fundamental assumption on which they all proceed, that some such judgments are true and others false, and that when any two

[1] Cf. Lecture IX.

such judgments conflict one or both must be erroneous. As before said, one fact cannot be inconsistent with another fact; accordingly, regarded from a psychological or sociological point of view, A's judgment, *e.g.* that all gambling is wrong, does not conflict with B's judgment that some gambling is right. The question, Which is true? does not arise and would have no meaning. The reduction therefore of Duty to Fact, on this line of thought, if strictly pursued, simply eviscerates ethical thought of its essential import and interest. The history of opinion is a most interesting branch of Sociology, but it has not in itself any criterion of the truth of opinion.

It may be replied, perhaps, that in this argument I have not taken into account the notions of life and development, and their place in psychology and sociology; that possessing these notions science, in this department, does not merely ascertain resemblances and general laws of co-existence and change, but in so doing brings out the notion of an end to which psychical and social changes are related as means, and in relation to which alone they are really intelligible; and that this end supplies the requisite reduction of 'what ought to be' to 'what is.' For in this end—variously conceived as vital or social 'health,' or 'equilibrium,' or 'life measured in breadth as well as length,'—we have, it is thought, a criterion of truth and error in moral judgments; if the acts men approve are conducive to this end they may be counted true or normal, if not false or abnormal.

To this I answer that End as a biological or sociological notion may, no doubt, be held convertible for practical purposes with ethical end, but that this can only be by an ethical judgment affirming the coincidence of the two: the two notions remain essentially distinct, though when affirmed to be coincident they are doubtless liable to be confused. From the mere knowledge that a certain result is what will be or preponderantly tends to be, it is impossible to infer that it ought to be. So far as it is inevitable, I obviously can have no duty with regard to it; so far as its coming may be promoted or retarded, it is my duty to promote it if I judge it good in comparison with that for which it would be substituted, and to retard it if I judge it to be comparatively bad. Perhaps I may suggest that this distinction between the two is often not clearly recognised, because in the terms, such as 'social welfare' or 'social health,' used to denote the sociological end, the ethical notion is surreptitiously introduced; they are states which have been implicitly judged to be good. And similarly we shall judge institutions and practices that cause misery now as bad on that ground, and not *merely* because they are not in the shortest line of progress to the future of humanity in which there will be—as Mr. Spencer seems to be convinced—"pleasure unalloyed by pain anywhere."[1]

§ 3. This leads me to another mode of establishing coherence between systematic thought about 'what

[1] [Cf. above, p. 189.]

is,' and systematic thought about what 'ought to be,' which belongs to a very different manner of thought, and yet is not without affinity with that just discussed —I mean the theological mode. It may, I think, be truly said that the problem which we are now discussing is the fundamental problem of Rational Theology. The task of Rational Theology is to bring our knowledge of what is into coherent relation to our systematic thought as to what ought to be, through the conception of God as a Being in whose righteous will what ought to be actually is. On this view the physical world is an effect and manifestation of Divine Power: the laws of phenomena, partially known by science, are a manifestation of Divine ordering intellect, while, on the other hand, what is thought to be good—provided it is truly thought— is the Divine End so far as revealed to us, and the fulfilment of the rules of Duty is the realisation of the Divine Will.

I have no intention or desire to dispute the truth of these momentous propositions, which, indeed, I regard as necessary assumptions for the religious consciousness. But I hold that they do not really solve the problem that we have now in view: they do not really enable us to bring our conceptions of 'what ought to be' and 'what is' into an intelligible relation of coherence. In considering this it will, I think, conduce to clearness to separate the conception of the Rules of Duty or Divine Commands, from the conception of Universal Good—*i.e.* what is truly thought to be such—as the Divine End.

Let us begin then with the theological assumption that the true rules of duty are Divine Commands—whether made known by external revelation or through the conscience of the individual. Such commands, it is said, may be imperfectly known to any particular moral agent, either without his own fault—in which case their non-fulfilment will be pardoned—or through wilful neglect of known duty in the past, which has had the effect of impairing his moral insight: but in any case such commands have been uttered, and must be regarded as a part of universal fact. Thus, it may be said, the conception of what ought to be may be brought under the general conception of what is. I think, however, that this reduction fails when we work it out. Firstly, we cannot define a Divine Command—like a human command — as wish *plus* threat, since we cannot attribute to God an ungratified wish. Shall we then conceive it as simply a threat? This would clearly offend Common Sense, which conceives God as not merely an Omnipotent Ruler, but also a Righteous Ruler, commanding in accordance with a Rule of Right. But thus the difference we are considering emerges again in the form of a distinction between the Rule of Right in the Divine Mind, and the Divine Power as manifested in the world of fact; and, emerging, it brings with it the formidable problem of the existence of evil; since we inevitably ask why God's power does not cause the complete realisation of ideal Right.

The answer of one section of theologians is that

God's purpose cannot be carried out without the creation of beings such as men endowed with Free Will: and that thus the endowment of Free Will renders the admission of wrong-doing inevitable. And so we are brought to the question of Free Will, which in the view of some is fundamentally important, not only in dealing with the relation of Practical to Theoretical Philosophy, but also in constructing Practical Philosophy itself.[1] My view of Free Will is nearly similar to Kant's—with the very important difference that he thinks that the antinomy or dilemma which we both recognise can be properly explained by taking the critical view of knowledge, whereas I hold that no satisfactory explanation has been found of it. I think the presumptive argument for regarding any particular human mind as an effect completely determined by pre-existing mundane causes is very strong, confirmed as it is by even the very imperfect success that we actually have in reducing its volitions to laws and foreseeing the particular volitions that will occur under particular circumstances. On the other hand, when I take the ethical view of action, I find it impossible to regard the volition, when wrong or imperfect, as completely determined in the moment of deliberate action by the causes to which, contemplating it after the event, I should refer to explain its wrongness or imperfection. To put it otherwise: I cannot regard absence of adequate

---

[1] I think its importance from the latter point of view has been exaggerated. Cf. *Methods of Ethics*, bk. I. ch. v. [where the subject of Free Will is more fully discussed].

motive as an obstacle to doing what I judge to be reasonable.[1]

But even granting the unqualified validity of this cognition of Freedom, the reconciliation is incomplete; as we see when we pass from considering Duty as Divine command to consider universal good as Divine End. For moral evil—wrong free choice—is in any case only a part of the world's evil. Physical Evil—not due to free choice—still remains in the world of living things. To deny its existence is violently paradoxical, and if it is admitted, I see no way of reconciling its existence with the goodness of God except by assuming that the Divine Will and Purpose work—like human will and purpose—under conditions. But in that case these conditions must be conceived as having some other source than the Divine Will—and then the theological synthesis of 'what ought to be' with 'what is' seems to fail, and the problem of bringing the two conceptions into coherent relation still awaits solution.

§ 4. This is not, however, the only important relation of Theology to Practical Philosophy. So far, for the sake of simplicity, I have assumed the task of Practical Philosophy—the reduction of our notions of what ought to be to a coherent system—to have been adequately accomplished. But what I have said elsewhere[2] of the conflict of self-interest and duty shows that this is not my view. Historically

---

[1] I introduce moral judgment because otherwise I feel no equally distinct impulse to reject determinism,

[2] *Methods of Ethics*, concluding chapter.

a fundamentally important result of Theism—and religion based on it—is the solution of this conflict. [But this presupposes the theoretic validity of Theism.][1]

I do not mean to imply that Theism is not self-evident or demonstrable. It clearly has been so regarded by very superior minds. When any one says, after Descartes, that finite being presupposes infinite being—not merely the idea of the infinite, but its actual existence, and, in particular, that in finite mental being, in finite intelligence and will, Infinite Intelligence and Will are presupposed, I think I understand, to some extent, the process of thought by which this affirmation is reached; and though I do not agree with it—holding rather that the finite only presupposes the infinite *in idea*—I do not see how the momentous difference between these two conclusions is to be settled by any argument.

I myself regard Theism as a belief which, though borne in upon the living mind through life, and essential to normal life, is not self-evident or capable of being cogently demonstrated. It belongs, therefore, to a class of beliefs which I do not dispute the general reasonableness of accepting, but which I think have to be considered carefully and apart in estimating the grounds of their acceptance—assumptions for which we cannot but *demand* further proof, though we may see no means of obtaining it. For there can be no doubt that one of the most important sources of human error lies in the accept-

[1] See *Methods of Ethics*, concluding chapter.

ance of traditions and suggestions incapable of being supported on adequate evidence.

Accordingly I think that our acceptance of such propositions must have a provisional character, as compared with those that are self-evident or demonstrated. I do not mean that in ordinary thought we are conscious of any material difference of certainty: at all events there is none in my own case, since the principle, *e.g.* of causality is in my view such a proposition. If any such assumption is confirmed by the test of consistency with other assumptions and cognitions of my own mind or of other minds, its certainty to me becomes, I think, practically indistinguishable from other certainty, though I recognise philosophically the provisional character of the structure of thought to which it belongs. The serious difficulty begins when such assumptions are divergent and conflicting. So far as this is the case, we must infer error in some or all of them, though we may believe the error to be useful, *i.e.* better adapted than truth would be for the life of certain minds. But the postulates of A can have no validity for B, who does not feel the need of them; on the other hand, B's recognition of their necessity for A must lead him to philosophic doubt of the objective validity of similar postulates in his own case.

§ 5. I do not say this as a mere spectator: as I am conscious of requiring for rational conduct such a postulate, namely, Moral order. This leads me to the connexion of Theism and Optimism (so far as Moral order goes). Neither, in my view involves the other. We may believe in Moral order—'the power not ourselves that makes for righteousness'—without connecting it with Personality. This is generally admitted. Perhaps it is less generally admitted that we may believe in Theism —in a Personal First Cause or ground of the finite universe—without believing in Moral order. But I go so far as to say that the chief abstract arguments (except one) used to prove Theism do not tend to prove Moral order.

Suppose it proved, in the Berkeleian or some other way, that Intelligent Will is the only real Cause, how is it proved that it has caused or will cause any other than the imperfect world that we know through experience? Supposing that we may legitimately infer a Designing Mind from the apparently designed result which the complex adjustments of living things present, what do we gain? When I infer human design from an effect, what I imagine and conceive to have pre-existed is a representation in idea in a certain mind, *approximately* similar in *important* points to the result produced. There *is* now in fact (say) a watch, there *was* therefore in idea a *represented* adjustment of matter more or less definitely *like* a watch in the important relations. The imperfection of resemblance may vary indefinitely in degree in human minds, but I cannot attribute any such indefiniteness to the Divine Design. If I infer Divine Design from the adjustments of a watch or of a living plant or animal, I must suppose the pre-existing idea—or let us omit pre-existing if the relations of time are denied of the Divine Thought —I must suppose the idea to be in every respect similar to the designed result; for the Divine Mind cannot be conceived to work, like the human mind, among material conditions and laws only partially comprehended. But then just in proportion to this perfection of resemblance is the absence of any explanatory efficacy in the reference of designed effect to designing cause. The design being in every particular and detail exactly like the effect, whatever difficulties we have in understanding how the latter came to be must recur with regard to the former; if I cannot prove moral order from the actual existence of the complexly adjusted world without referring it to a designing Mind, I do not see how it is any more to be proved, after the reference has been made, from the ideal existence of an exactly similar world. We have merely duplicated the actual world; we have a world in idea, existing previously to, or apart from, the actual, but presenting exactly the same difficulties from its apparent imperfections. The inferred design affords no more evidence of Moral order than the designed effect from which it is inferred.

§ 6. But, finally, I think that Philosophy can reduce somewhat the difference between 'what is,' and what 'ought to be,' since the difference between two things compared is reduced by discovering previously unknown resemblances between them, although the notions still remain essentially distinct. *E.g.* we may compare the circle and the parabola without knowing that they are both sections of the cone. Surely we should say that the difference between them ascertained by this comparison is reduced by discovering their common relation to the cone? If so, I think it must be admitted that this kind of 'reduction' takes place when we contemplate the difference between 'what is' and 'what ought to be' from a philosophical or epistemological point of view. For from this point of view we regard the world of Duty and the world of Fact as objects of thought and—real or supposed—knowledge, and discover similar relations of thought in both, relations of universal to particular and individual notions and judgments, of inductive to deductive method, etc. Whatever differences may appear between the two from this point of view are of a subordinate kind, and not greater than the differences between different departments of Fact regarded as objects of thought and scientific method. True, if we adhere to Common Sense, the fundamental difference remains that the distinction beween 'truth' and 'error,' in our thought about 'what is,' is held to depend essentially on the correspondence or want of correspondence between Thought and Fact; whereas in the case of 'what ought to be,' truth and error cannot be conceived to depend on any similar relation. Still even this difference is at least reduced if we take the philosophical point of view, because from this point of view the supposed correspondence between Thought and what is not Thought is no longer so simple and intelligible as it seems to Common Sense;

though it must be admitted to be a difficult problem, whatever solution of it we may ultimately accept. Further, we must recognise that even in the case of our thought about 'what is,' though error may lie in want of correspondence between Thought and Fact, it can only be ascertained and exposed by showing inconsistency between Thought and Thought, *i.e.* precisely as error is disclosed in the case of our Thought about 'what ought to be.'[1]

[1] [Cf. above Lecture II. pp. 33 f.]

INDEX

Absolute, 96-98; Being, 39, 124; truth, 178-179, 190-191
Æsthetics, 35
Agnosticism, 15, 94, 103
Agreement of experts, *see* Consensus
Analysis, 151; three methods of, 63, 81
Antecedents not elements in Psychology, 71, 150
Appearance, 14-16, 93, 100, 104, 117
Aristotle, 1, 80, 94, 226

Balfour, Mr. A. J., defines philosophy, 110
Beauty, as good in itself, 29
Beginning of world in Time, 84, 85, 91
Belief, origin and validity of, 152, 172; common, 161; department of Sociology, 160; criterion of, 105, 111-113; negative and destructive effect of historical study on, 162-171, 173-174; constructive, 174-179, Lectures IX., X.
Biology, 25; method in, 56; historical method in, 133-149
Botany, 7, 133

Causal nexus in Psycho-physiology, 54
Causation, sciences of, 8
Cause, First, 39, 228
Classification, Sciences of, 7, 8
Coherence a test of truth, 99, 219
Common Sense, 42, 43; view of Mind, 44; not overthrown by Psychogonical analysis, 71-75; in Ethics, 172
Comte, Auguste; Positive Philosophy, 80, *note*; "social factor," 153; influence on Mill, 153, 160, *note*; law of the three stages, 168, 194, 218, 225-229; monogamy, 170; regards whole human race, 216
Consensus of Experts, lacking in philosophy, 5, 13; destroys sceptical effect of historical method, 173; a note of Science, 217; a test of truth, 219
Constructive effect of historical method, 162, 174
Continuity, Argument from, 145-148; of Development in Science, 217
Controversy in Science and between Sciences, 106-107; in Ethics, Politics, Theology, 190, 219
Copernicus, 100, 108
Creation, Special, 136-139
Criterion of truth, 105; not from Sociology, 205; Philosophy, 111; Logic and Epistemology, 112; no general criterion of material truth, 114; Logic and Metaphysic in Mill, 115; Ontology, 117
Cyclical course of changes, 198

Darwinism, 108, 133; and the general conception of Evolution, 136-139; and immortality of soul consistent, 143
Descartes; quantum of matter unchangeable known *à priori*, 84; his scepticism, 109; physical science not indubitable as for us, 196
Design, *see* Teleology
Destructive effect of Sociology, 162-174
Development, 186
Dialectical method, 49
Difference, systematic, 18
Dualism, 120-121; Natural Dualism, *see* Common Sense
Duty, world of, 234

Ego, 86
Empirical Reflective Analysis, 63, 81; Verification, 83, 89, 99
Empiricism, 92, 119, *note*
End, 198; three meanings of, 201; in Sociology, 186, 237; in the Arts

28-29; in Practical Philosophy, 30; excluded from Science, 225
Epistemology, 4, 105; its primary aim, 109; and Ontology, 111-112, 117; and Logic, 112-117; Külpe's view, 119-121; and historical method, 156
Error in antecedents of a belief, 167, 174
Ethics, 4, 24, 35; its aim, 25; and Politics, 27; and Practical Philosophy, 27, 31; and Geometry, 34, *note*; historical study important, 162
Evil, 30, 38 f., 233
Evolution, Mr. Spencer's doctrine, 19; and psychogonical analysis, 69; distinct from Darwinism, 136
Extension, 70

"Faces of the same thing," Mind and Matter not, 53
Feeling, in older English sense, 45; peculiar matter of Psychology, 46; Sensationalism, 63; and knowledge, 148
First Cause, 39, 228
Foresight, sociological, a difficulty, 177, 180
Formal Truth, 113-114
Freedom, 56, 240 f.

Galileo, 19, 108
Generality, the characteristic of Science, 8
Geography, 7
Geometrical Solidity, 69
Geometry and Ethics, 34, *note*
God, 38-39, 94
Good, 95, 283
Gratitude, duty of, 176
Gravitation, law of, 9, 74
Greece, changes in belief, 207
Green, T. H., 96, 103

Hamilton, Sir W., 69; on Theoretical and Practical Philosophy, 32; Philosophy as Science of Mind, 35
Hegel's work metaphysical, 89
Heredity, 69
Heterogeneity and homogeneity, 130-133
Historical Method, as dominant, 124; and Inductive Method, 126; in Mathematics, 127; in Rational Physics, 128; and the particularity of the cosmos, 129-133; in Zoology, 133; in Sociology, 137; Materialism *v.* Spiritualism, 142-143; and Immortality, 143-149;
wider and narrower sense, 157; and Scepticism, 164-171, 173-174
History, 4, *note*, 7; ancient view of, 122-123; new view of, 124
Hylozoism, 147

Idealism, 60, 62, 103; and Realism in Külpe, 119
Immortality, 143-149
Improvement, 211, 214
Incompressibility, 69
Individual and Society (Mill), 153-154
Inductive and Historical methods, 126
Inference, 82, 114
Infinite extension of the world, 84, 85
Innate and Intuitive, 151, 164
Introspection, 49, 86-87, 151; for Kant, 103
Intuition, 151, 164; of Self, 86

Jurisprudence, 23, 25

Kant, 81, 85, 92, 102-103
Kantian Logicians, 113-114
Kelvin, vortex theory, 74
Kepler, 19, 165
Knowledge and feeling, 148
Külpe, 4; on Epistemology, 119

Law of the three Stages, *see* Comte
Logic, 4, 35, 82, 112; Kantian, 113; Mill, 114; and Epistemology, 117

Man, Science of, 35
Material truth, 113-114
Materialism, 9, 36, 41, 42, 52, 54, 60, 61, 76; in Külpe, 121; and Biological Evolution, 142; and Sensationalism, 150
Mathematics, 8, 127
Matter, related to Mind, 60; Philosophy and Psychology, 51 f.; analysis of notion, 63-75
Mentalism, 41, 61, 103
Metaphysics, 39, 77; thought futile, 78, 195, 218; and Physics, 82; and Psychology, 86; and Philosophy, 87; Transcendental, 91; and Theology, 94; and Logic, 113-118; in Külpe, 119-121; and Sociology, 179
Method, no universal, 220
Methodology, 102, 116
Mill, J. S., 31, *note*; definition of Philosophy, 35; of Logic, 82, 114; the "social factor," 153-154, 159,

INDEX 251

160 ; on Theological explanation, 222
Mind, Science of, 35 ; relation to Matter, 51, 60 ; studied teleologically, 229
Monism, Materialistic, 121
Monotheism and Polytheism (Comte), 227
Motion, Laws of, 18, 87

Natural Philosophy, 2, 6 ; Dualism, see Common Sense
Naturalistic Philosophy, 24, 76
Nature non-ethical, 224 ; antiteleological, 225

Ontology, 96, 100, *note*, 112, 117-121
Organism, Society as, 201

Particularity of cosmos, 132
Perception, 60
Periodic course of changes, 198
Phenomena, 14, 17, 21
Phenomenalism, 62
Philosophy, and Science, 4-11 ; its aim, 12 ; Practical, 21-35, 232 ff., as Science of Man, 35 ; method, 49 ; non-metaphysical, 87-90
Physics, 8 ; philosophical, 9 ; and metaphysics, 82-85 ; reality and appearance, 98 ; historical method, 128-129, 140-141
Physiology, 52-59, 73
Plato, Theology in, 94
Political Philosophy, 2, 22, 26
Politics, 24, 26, 27, 31, 35, 106, 162
Polytheism, Comte on, 227
Positive, Science, 21 ; Philosophy, 24, 26, 76
Practical, Philosophy, 22-35, Lect. XII. ; Reason, 225
Preservation as the sociological end, 186, 202, 210
Pro-ethical sentiments ; Revenge, 170
Progress, 197 ; not necessarily preservative, 203 ; in belief, 205
Progressivism, 178, 190, 212 ; combined with philosophical relativism, 195
Psychogonical analysis, 63, 69, 149
Psychological Philosophy, 47, 76
Psychology, 4, 24, 35 ; and Philosophy, 41, 44 f. ; relation to Matter, 44 ; Feeling, peculiar subject-matter of, 46 ; and Beliefs, 45, 48 ; and Sociology, 51 ; and Physiology, 52-59 ; and

Metaphysics, 81, 85, 86-87 ; and historical method, 149-152
Punishment, 168

Reality and Appearance, 15, 22, 92, 96, 100, *note*, 104, 117
Relative knowledge, 96 f., 178, 182-189, 191
Relativism, 190, 195, 212
Religion, 38 ; as social force, 209
Roman Empire, 204, 208

Scepticism and the Historic Method, 163, 176 ; its limits, 196
Science and Philosophy, 2, 3, 4, 11 ; of Classification, 7 ; of Causation, 8 ; "generality," 8 ; of phenomena, 14-17 ; Positive, 21 ; and Theoretical Philosophy, 30-31 ; of Man, 35 ; and Theology and Metaphysics, 221-230
Secondary qualities, 64
Self, 86
Sensationalism, 42, 62 ; inconsistent, 72, 150
Sense-perception, verification by, 88, 99
Society an organism, 201 ; and the Individual (Mill), 153
Sociological method, 157 ; foresight, 177, 180 ; end, 186, 202
Sociology, 25, 35-36 ; and Psychology, 51, 81, 152, 158-161 ; and Philosophy, 189, 230 ; and scepticism, 163-174 ; and Metaphysics, 179 ; constructive effect, 174
Solidity, geometrical, 69 ; physical, 69, 70
Space, 151 ; the Transcendentalist view, 92, 102-104
Spencer, Mr. Herbert ; Definition of Philosophy, 13, 17, 38, 105 ; Agnosticism, 14, 16, 22, 79, 221 ; Evolution, 19, 130 ; Science, 21, 31 ; Ethics, 23 ; Psychology, 36 ; disparateness of Mind and Matter, 53, 142-143 ; and Materialism, 72 ; and Metaphysics, 80, *note*, 88, 96, 221 ; "pro-ethical" sentiments, 170 ; Comte's Sociology different, 216 ; optimism 224
Spiritualism, 142
Stephen, Mr. Leslie, on Sociology, 110

Teleology, 94, 227
Theism, 242 ; and Moral Order, 243 f.
Theology, 38, 94 ; controversy, 106 ; a form of error, 195, 218 ; and Science,

223 ; Rational, its problem, 38, 94, 238
Theoretical Philosophy, 26 ; its relation to Practical, 232 ff.
Time, the Transcendental view, 92, 102-104
Transcendental analysis, 63, 91, 102-104

Verification, empirical, 83, 89, 99, 118
Volitional explanation, 222
Vortex-ring theory, 85

Welfare, as end, 186
Wissenschaft, 4, *note*

Zoology, 7, 133

THE END

Printed by R. & R. CLARK, LIMITED, *Edinburgh*